A Legacy *of Lies*

A Legacy of Lies
A Woman's Journey to the Truth

By Jeanne Hall

A Legacy of Lies:
A Woman's Journey to the Truth
Copyright © 2015 by Jeanne Hall

All rights reserved. No part of this book may be used or reproduced in any manner whatsoever including Internet usage, without written permission of the author.

Editor: Claudia Reynolds

Cover Design: Foundry 43 Creative Studio, Nashville, TN
Front Cover Photograph: Dottie Hall
Back Cover Photograph: Dixie Gamble

Book design by Maureen Cutajar
www.gopublished.com

DEDICATED TO MAMA
*May the telling of our story soothe your soul
And bring you Peace.*

Acknowledgements

No one walks their life journey alone, no matter how alone we may feel at times. There is always someone to catch us when we fall. In my case, I have fallen so many times that I may have difficulty remembering everyone who helped me up. If you do not find yourself on this page, please know that you are in my heart.

Thank you Claudia Reynolds, my beautiful and compassionate editor. Your encouragement and kind words were priceless. Ryan Wagner, your gentleness and artistry has graced me. Candy Paull, thank you for sharing your knowledge and for answering my endless questions. Pam Lewis of PLA Media, thanks for my title. Jana Stanfield, thanks for your heart and your amazing marketing mind.

To all my Sistahs, who have seen me at my worst and still called me friend, you are my Soul Mates. Thanks for floating naked in the pool with me while shielding ourselves with umbrellas from a midnight Southern California rainstorm. Yvonne Kelly & Koko Zamoyski, thanks for listening and listening and listening. Tanya Tarver, thanks for showing up when I least expected you but really needed you. My other dear, dear Tonya Conway, life long friend and supporter, thanks for always finding me. Margo Fisher, thank you for your wonderful sense of humor. Dixie Gamble, thanks for your love and for reading my early manuscript. Pam Rose & Mary Ann Kennedy, you have blessed me with your music, your kindness and great generosity. Janet Duckham and Cindy Gough, you bring me such great joy. My Soul Sistah, Jill Colucci, there is No One Else On Earth. You have housed me, fed me & loved me. There are no words.

To my beautiful, loving family, I was born under a Lucky Star to have been graced by your presence in my life. Mimi & Pappy, you have always been my safe place. I love you deeply. Mike & Ridge, you are my brothers! Maggie, thank you for your generosity and understanding. Sherry, thank you for your steadiness. To my sweet sister-in-law Bonnie, thanks for your love & care. To my brother Bill, you have always managed to make me laugh and I am grateful for that. For my brother Jim, thank you for being our champion. Thank you for being the one person on this planet who understands the depth of the love we shared for our Daddy. You have become the man Mama dreamed you could be. Aunt Dottie, you are my hero. To all my courageous cousins and those not so brave, thanks, we are free!

I have loved and been loved by so many in my life. I feel your presence everyday in every way! Most of all, I am graced by the love of God, Spirit, Higher Power, The Great Creator, all the Forces within the Universe. You have always been the wind beneath my wings.

Contents

Chapter One	In the Beginning: Mama	1
Chapter Two	Then There Was Light: Daddy	21
Chapter Three	Into the Red Sea: A Bad, Wrong Turn	34
Chapter Four	Judas: The Betrayal	40
Chapter Five	Life A.D.	44
Chapter Six	Life Continues A.D.	58
Chapter Seven	The Deadly Serpent Appears	78
Chapter Eight	Out of the Wilderness	98
Chapter Nine	Sodom and Gomorrah	112
Chapter Ten	The Garden of Eden	153
Chapter Eleven	It Is Finished	167
Chapter Twelve	Revelations at Last	178
Chapter Thirteen	The Omega Becomes the Alpha	190
Chapter Fourteen	Armageddon Leads to New Beginnings	198

One

IN THE BEGINNING: MAMA

It is a simple story yet all of life is in the telling. Its enigmas have mystified me and often led my fragmented mind to diversion and deep despair. As each of us seeks to unravel our own mysteries, I wonder if there is a deeper challenge or a greater joy than those shared between a mother and a daughter. There are none as deep, as complicated, as hurtful, as helpful, as nurturing, as damaging, as encouraging, as defeating, as loving, as despising nor as eternal. No matter the number of friends, family, lovers, or acquaintances we meet along our journeys, none matches the impression or guides our way with equal impact. It is a journey each of us is required to take. It is a journey we must travel on our own.

My brother Jim and I were both born in the small Southern town of Albany, Georgia. In the springtime large magnolia trees blossomed sprinkling the neighborhoods with their lovely white bouquets. Yellow daffodils filled the air with their sanguine fragrance. The summers brought Spanish moss that hung high from large oak trees and swayed in the summer breezes. We walked barefoot skipping along unpaved roads and rode our bicycles to the nearby creek where we scavenged for crayfish. There was a sweetness that pervaded our lives. Appearances were paramount, silence was golden, secrets were hidden, and gossip shared. There was an unstated proper order to this tranquil life. It was not to be disturbed.

My brother Jim still lives in our hometown, although we both acknowledge that with the passage of time and the increase of population, it has lost much of its charm and allure. On those rare occasions when I visit him, we enjoy our time together and have grown closer with each afternoon spent. On one such occasion, we took a drive to our childhood neighborhood as we often did. We traced our steps, winding through the now-paved roads and marveled at the newly built small town mansions that occupied the land where we once stood barefoot in the cold creek water. While recalling the romance of the "good ole days," I made an off-hand, rather innocuous remark about our grandfather. I was highly amused as was Jim and we shared a chuckle at Granddaddy's expense. I thought nothing further of it.

The following day we sat together in the Albany airport as we waited for the plane that would return me to my current home in Nashville, TN. I had spent many hours there while awaiting planes to return me to my previous homes in New York City and Los Angeles, CA. The runway and the lobby looked eerily the same as it did all those years before when I first encountered the FBI, Dr. Martin Luther King, and his wife, Coretta. In an instant, I was back in the excitement and frantic atmosphere of that earlier afternoon. I quickly returned to present day as Jim and I chatted nonchalantly and without concern.

Suddenly he grew quiet and out of this serenity, he shook my world. With eyes widened and quickened breath Jim remarked: "You know, I grew up in the same house with you, and I never saw anything with Granddaddy. I need some evidence."

I was stunned. Jim and I had not mentioned our grandfather's name in years. I realized that his inquiry had been sparked by my humorous

In The Beginning: Mama

comment the previous afternoon. Clearly Jim felt that if he had not seen anything, then it did not actually exist. This realization touched me to the core.

"I am your evidence," I simply replied.

"It is not enough. I need more," he said with a coldness in his voice.

I fought back my tears, determined to shield my hurt from his repudiation. Shortly I heard the muddled sound of the announcer over the PA system calling for my flight to board. I headed to the security check as Jim and I said our goodbyes. I boarded the plane in an altered state.

For the duration of my flight I gazed out from my portal as we sped high above the perfectly squared farm land, the multiple flowing rivers, and the magnificent red Georgia clay that lay below us. I pondered my brother's skepticism as the beauty below served to balance the pain I felt inside. My mind traveled to my earliest recollections of life with Jim and our family.

Our mother, for whom I was named, but known only to us as Mama, was the first of nine daughters born to my grandparents. They lived on a farm in a small Georgia town, population three-hundred. Her beauty lay in her dark, haunting eyes that glared out with wonder and softened with sadness. Her hands were beautiful, radiating a sense of power and character about them. They were working hands. They were giving hands. They were loving hands, gentle to the touch.

Mama's family lived in a rambling old house complete with a front porch and a swing that made a haunting squeaky noise with each passing turn. In the yard was a towering oak tree whose roots bulged out of the earth making it hard to run around, yet perfect for climbing and hiding from the unwanted advances of any male cousins. High on one of the sturdiest of limbs, a hemp rope was wrapped around an old, worn rubber tire that served as the children's swing. I can still feel the wind on my warm face and the race of my heart as I soared higher and higher into the air, hoping the breeze would lift me up to fly with the birds.

The wire fence had turned red with rust from years of rain and sweltering hot summers. As each screaming child passed in and out of the house, the screen door made a unique, slapping sound as it slammed against the doorframe. In the summer when the air was heavy with humidity, the women sat on the porch cooling themselves with paper fans attached to wooden sticks. On one side was a pretty picture of a church and on the other an advertisement for the local funeral parlor. I never quite understood their message. If you don't go to church, you're going to need this fan where you're going? And we'll be happy to take you there? Nonetheless, while on this earth, those fans kept many a fine, Southern lady from fainting and falling onto the floor in a most unladylike manner.

As children, we spent most of our holidays and many summer vacations in this little country town. Often it was at our grandparents' farm, and not where we wanted to be.

Mama persistently said, "This could be your grandma and granddaddy's last Christmas," (or their last birthday...or their last Fourth of July). "So we're going. Get in the car."

I remember frequently rolling my eyes when this "last whatever it was" conversation began. Then, as planned, Jim and I reluctantly hopped into the car for the short drive to their farm. In hindsight, this is really quite charming as Grandma lived to be 101-years-old.

A cornfield and wild blackberry bushes separated their house from the railroad tracks. As children we were awakened by the train's haunting whistle piercing the stillness of the night. That sound still arouses in me a deep feeling of loneliness that is unmatched to this day.

The tracks did however provide some joyful moments. All the cousins would travel in groups through the fields, weaving in and out of the corn stalks while gathering wild berries as we went. Our blue

In The Beginning: Mama

tongues and fingers were an accurate substantiation of the adventure. Very few of those berries made it back to Grandma's kitchen. Those that did happily found themselves in a homemade blackberry cobbler topped with fresh vanilla ice cream.

Summers in the Deep South were filled with heat, humidity, air so heavy it became visible, and steam that billowed up from the pavement. As we chased each other around the coarsely graveled front yard or swung from the old oak tree, sweat ran down our faces, oozed from our pores, and dripped off the hairs on the backs of our necks. The only respite from this smothering, oppressive heat was to put our skinny, young bodies into our swimsuits and head to Nantze Springs. The natural spring water bubbled up from deep in the earth and made for a chilling, breathtaking summer adventure. The contrast between the cold water and the humid, heavy air shocked our systems though none of us hesitated from jumping in with great fervor. As we chatted to each other our voices vibrated from the force of our skinny, shaking bodies. Wrapped in our tattered cotton towels, we stood shivering, speaking with our purple lips, and gesturing with our shriveled up prune fingers. After a few short moments, off we would go back into the frigid cold for more blissful, intoxicating summertime fun.

Grandma was a quiet, kind woman who kept to herself and stayed primarily in her domain, the kitchen. She seemed to gain a certain sense of power there. Although it was the center of most of the activity for these large events, it nonetheless appeared to be a place of peace for her. At family reunions, all her nine daughters gathered there as they arrived with their fried chicken, sweet potato pies, freshly cooked field peas, lima beans, and baked hams. The aroma of these uniquely Southern delicacies floated throughout the house and awakened the appetite of all those within range of it.

Grandma's first order of business was to prepare her world-renowned recipe for homemade rolls. She made beautiful dough with just the perfect consistency. Then, using her wooden roller, she'd press it out on a sheet of waxed paper. All the years that I watched her cutting the dough into small circles, she used the same bent, worn aluminum cutter with a red handle that had faded with time. At this point, if you had won her favor or were just lucky enough to be passing by, you were asked to participate in the traditional ritual of dunking each roll into a pot of freshly melted butter. With each drip on the table we would shriek with delight knowing we had been a part of an extraordinary experience. I have come to realize that perhaps some of the hips on my Mother's sisters may have gotten their start right there in that kitchen with those butter dipped delights.

Above the clattering of pots and pans, the oven doors slamming, the overly-exaggerated greetings, and the shouts of dismay, there was one sound that traveled throughout the house and reverberated off the walls in each room. It was laughter. I can truly say that I learned how to laugh right there in that small, over-crowded kitchen in the company of a woman I loved and yet never quite understood or even felt close to.

In her later years, Grandma was missing several of her front teeth. When she shyly smiled she covered her mouth with her hands as if to hide the glaring holes from the viewer. This malady, however, did not keep her from proudly participating in one of her greatest loves, music. In the tiny living room, crowded with over-stuffed sofas and chairs, was a large upright, usually out-of-tune, piano. Its presence there signified its importance in the household. The keys were yellowed with age, and those that remained were often worn to the wood from years of use and misuse at the hands of the twenty-five, or so, grandchildren who were given free rein of the house.

During every family gathering, no matter the occasion, eventually Grandma would find herself sitting at that ole piano. Having had no formal training, she played strictly by ear. There were no subtleties to her performances, yet all were filled with passion and a deep love of the art. At the sound of the first notes, word rippled throughout the house that our presence was required at the impending event. No ex-

In The Beginning: Mama

ceptions. We all gathered 'round to sing our favorite Church hymns like "The Little Brown Church In The Vale," " Shall We Gather At The River," "The Old Rugged Cross"—those haunting old melodies that grab your heart, no matter how callous, and make you have a comin'-to-Jesus moment. Grandma pounded the keys. Uncle Jack pierced the air with his out of tune notes. Mama sang like an opera star. All the kids rolled their eyes in sheer pain at having to participate. Men mumbled under their breath, cousins giggled, everyone laughed. In those fleeting moments there was a lovely sense of family and a rare feeling of well-being. Strangely, however, I don't recall ever having seen my granddaddy sharing in the joy of this family ritual.

The back yard of their house was mostly dirt where the chickens and the rooster had their way. Although they had indoor plumbing, for some reason, all the debris from the kitchen sink emptied directly into a hand-dug ditch in the backyard that ran the length of the house. Milk, softened pieces of bread, and the fruit from a near by fig tree drifted by. This outdoor drainage ditch became the watering hole for any and all farm animals—chicks, pigs, loose horses, and even cat-sized rats. It was fertile ground for a multitude of bacteria and oddly fragrant odors.

Granddaddy was a small-framed man with gray hair and rounded shoulders. His most distinguishing features were the yellow stains on his index and third fingers. He acquired these by rolling his own cigarettes from Prince Albert tobacco that he carried in a red tin can in his back pocket. After carefully rolling the cigarette, Granddaddy would lightly lick it with his tongue to make the paper stick together. Then he'd strike a stick match on the heel of his shoe to light it. Oddly enough, as a young adult rolling my first marijuana joint, I felt quite at ease with the technique as I had remembered those occasions as a child watching my granddaddy roll his Prince Albert.

As children we were most fascinated by the red tin can in the back pocket. Often we snuck inside to find the yellow pages of the local phone book. There we would search for the number of a nearby grocery store and call them.

"Do you have Prince Albert in the can?" we asked in our most adult voices.

To our delight, if the answer was "Yes," we'd giggle and say, "Well, you'd better let him out."

We were not the first nor will we be the last to make this inquiry. Small town store owners have been answering this question since the Prince was first introduced to the public in the early twentieth century.

I do not have a memory of Granddaddy ever going to work, tilling the soil, feeding the horses, or planting the seeds. In fact, I never really saw him do anything except walk up to the corner grocery store. There he would sit with the other local farmers smoking their cigarettes and talking about the weather. Later in the afternoon he'd amble up the clay dirt road to the house where a fresh home-cooked supper would be waiting as always. I often wondered if he was bored with this lifestyle. Did he feel fulfilled? Was he happy? Or was he content with things just the way they were?

When a summer rain blew by, as it often did, the Georgia clay turned to red mud. The force of the cars traveling over the back roads dug deep washboard holes into the earth. As children we loved to ride over them, screaming as our voices vibrated from the motion. It was better than a ride at the county fair, and we could enjoy it for free. It was such a simple life.

Not so for my mother who was the firstborn child of my grandparents. By all accounts it was a hard life. Grandma birthed eleven children—ten girls and one boy who was stillborn. In my mind that lone, little boy thought he wouldn't be able to survive with all that female energy, so he just decided to skip this lifetime. One of the baby girls died, after only three weeks of life, leaving nine surviving daughters. In my mother's eyes, Grandma was perpetually pregnant. All eleven children that she birthed, including the two that did not survive, appeared one after the other in rapid succession. As the first

In The Beginning: Mama

born, it became Mama's responsibility to care for her younger siblings. Although two of them were born after Mama left the house, for the most part, she fed them, changed their diapers and babysat them for all of her childhood years.

I don't recall intimate conversations between the sisters, yet there was a strange, unspoken support and caring for each other. Whenever any number of them were together, there was nonstop laughter, loud voices, some bossy attitudes, and a genuine affection exhibited among them. Of course, if all nine were present in the same location, cameras flashed as though the paparazzi were chasing the newest young Hollywood starlet. These photographs of multiple hairstyles and outfits illustrate the family history and the changing times.

Although they grew up in the same environment, each had their own very distinct personality. Strong wills and determination were traits many of them shared. Even as a child, however, I saw a sadness and a vulnerability in each that I found strangely eerie. I now understand that my discomfort stemmed from my ability to tap into that same sadness and vulnerability within my own heart. We shared something. I came to cherish each of the sisters in very unique ways.

During those years, since Granddaddy was not a working man, there was often very little food on the table. Sometimes dinner was cold biscuits left over from breakfast along with a warm glass of water. Winters were particularly hard, as coal heat and sweaters were luxuries. During the summer rains, the tin roof leaked, leaving behind only the smothering mugginess that is found so readily in that part of the South. It literally choked the breath out of my mother and opened the door for a lifetime of sadness and a deep sense of loss, a loss she spent her life struggling to recover. She often told me that she could hardly wait to get out of that house. She ran away and married her first husband when she was seventeen.

The greatest gift I ever gave my mother was being born on her forty-second birthday. She had already given birth to two sons by her first husband and another son by her second husband, my father. She and Daddy lived in Albany, Georgia, the largest "city" in the southwest corner of the state, population 35,000. There was one small hospital, Phoebe Putney Memorial. It supplied the needs of all the surrounding little farm towns and country folks.

Mama often told the story of arriving for her annual physical feeling lethargic, thinking perhaps she was anemic. After a thorough examination, the doctor was happy to inform her that she was perfectly healthy and perfectly pregnant. She recalls standing up with her hands on her hips, glaring into the eyes of the rather large Dr. Neil and announcing with vehemence,

"I am *not* pregnant and I am *not* having another child at my age."

Dr. Neil simply smiled and left the room with a chuckle. Seven months later, I arrived as a birthday gift at 6:30 on a Monday morning. Mama recalls looking across the crowded operating room. A nurse held me up for her to see. When she first saw my rosy cheeks and lips, she realized it had all been worth it. After twenty-five years of longing, she had finally given birth to "her little girl." She loved to tell this story, and did so often.

I am relatively certain that while in her womb I sensed her disgust at the thought of my arriving into her world. This recognition set the pattern for a lifetime challenge of feeling unwanted and quite out-of-sync with the world and my surroundings. I demonstrated my own disgust and disdain by refusing to assimilate the milk from her own body. No matter what the doctors tried with her breast milk, somehow it was much too unpleasant for my tiny stomach, and finally, right before I starved myself to death, Dr. Neil put me on Similac. I am certain in my tiny mind I was thinking, "You didn't want me—I don't want you." Thus began our life long love-hate, butting-heads relationship. It still astounds me that it is possible to so deeply despise and distrust someone and, at the very same time, so deeply love and want to please that same person.

In the South during this time period, it was rare for a woman to have a child in her forties. In fact, it was frowned upon and was accompanied by a certain amount of shame. I suspect it was this societal

In The Beginning: Mama

pressure that made my impending birth such a challenge for my mother. Her shame surely was also compounded by her own puritanical and rigid views of sex. What greater embarrassment than announcing to the world by your bulging belly that you were still engaging in sexual activity at the age of forty-one. As a child I often remember Mama covering her mouth and whispering, "She's PG," when referring to a pregnant woman no matter her age. In fact, I don't recall ever hearing the word pregnant until I went away to college in the 1960s.

Mama was not the only one who had trepidations about my entry into our tight-knit family. My brother Jim had been the recipient of all the love and attention that Mama and Daddy had to offer for twenty-one months. He enjoyed the adoration and wanted no intruders. Then I came along to rock his world and shift the balance of power. One day, while comfortably napping in my beautifully laced crib, adorned in a matching white dress and bonnet, Jim snuck into my parents' room as I slept. Without hesitation, he dumped me and my little white dress onto the hardwood floor. There was no mistaking his feelings about his new baby sister. If this were to happen in a family today, I am relatively certain that little Jimmy would have been whisked off to a few sessions of therapy to discuss his "issues." When you think about it for a moment, however, he made his "issue" known in a most aggressive and certain manner. It was clearly me.

Over the years I often heard Mama remark that I rarely cried as a child. From the day they brought me home from the hospital, I frequently slept through the night or otherwise laid quietly in my crib. She thought perhaps that somewhere in my tiny, baby life, I knew that she and Daddy were older and needed their sleep. I am not certain of my motives, however, I do have a cellular memory of these events, and the fear of reprisal for disturbing the peace of others has been a lifelong challenge. This fear has cost me a great deal of cash and has certainly paid the mortgages for more than one therapist through the years.

Our rented house was on Madison Street near Jefferson. It was so

All-American, charming and simple. Although it was not the best neighborhood, I did not know nor did I care. It was home to me. The front porch was concrete and brick. Mama grew red and white geraniums in large clay pots that lined the steps. She loved flowers and all varieties of birds. Each Spring she grew long-stemmed hollyhock plants outside the kitchen door. The blooming array of rich colors and fragrances seemed to bring her solace as she prepared our daily meals.

There wasn't a better cook anywhere in the South. Her fried chicken was unmatched. Her success was primarily attributed to her two well-kept secrets. First, put only Gold Medal Self-Rising White Flour in a brown paper bag, add just the perfect salt to pepper ratio, drop the freshly butchered bird into the bag, and shake until just the right consistency of flour stuck to the moist pieces. The second secret, critical to her success, was the temperature of the hot Crisco lard now cooking in her wrought iron frying pan. If it was too hot, the outside burned and the inside was raw. If it was too cool, all the moisture was cooked out, leaving it tough and tasteless. I watched her hundreds of times and have never mastered the technique. Therefore, I have never tasted fried chicken as moist, juicy and crispy as hers.

I fondly remember many times sitting at the dinner table after a meal of fresh collard greens, fried okra, homemade corn pones, field peas, and freshly brewed sweet iced tea. Just to clarify, it was considered blasphemous to have even thought about unsweetened iced tea or tea sweetened with anything other than pure cane sugar. After this delicious meal Mama would ask if anyone wanted dessert. Of course, the answer was a resounding "yes." She left the table, went into the kitchen, rolled out a pie crust from scratch, and threw in some locally grown Georgia peaches. Within minutes, we had a hot homemade peach cobbler topped with Kinnett's Vanilla Ice Cream.

Cooking and caring for us was Mama's job. It was an extension of her. It flowed from her as naturally as the Flint River in downtown Albany ambled to the Gulf of Mexico and the hummingbirds fluttered to her hollyhock blossoms. As a child, I accepted and expected it

In The Beginning: Mama

every day. I rarely thought to ask if she needed help, if she was bored, or if she was tired. It was her life. I don't believe she ever thought to question it either. It just was.

Our house was built off the ground with sturdy brick pillars at each corner. This was a familiar architecture during the forties and fifties, especially since we lived near the riverfront. Having the house uplifted made for many intriguing hiding places and afforded more creativity in our imaginary game playing. The dark and dampness also provided us with more creepy, crawly creatures to entertain us. One of our favorite games was playing doodlebug. The only apparatus needed in order to participate was a tiny stick found anywhere in the backyard. The doodlebugs were gray in color with hundreds of tiny little legs extending from their leathery textured bodies. They made holes in the dark, sandy soil that left two-inch mounds protruding from the earth that immediately gave away their secret protective hiding places. We circled the mounds with our sticks, singing "Doodle bug, doodle bug, come out tonight." When we finally did uncover the tiny creatures burrowing into the earth, they rolled into tight balls to protect themselves from the savage predators that we were. These tiny gray creatures were surely drunk from the motion as they were turned into miniature beach balls to be tossed back and forth between us.

Once Mama got used to the idea of having her "long-awaited" daughter, she seemed to relish in the thought. In her vision I would be dainty with pale skin, feminine, have pursed lips, love to play with dolls, and do girly things. In reality I was none of these. I actually don't recall ever playing with dolls, although I have evidence to the contrary as witnessed by my favorite picture of myself as a child. I have on a little brown skirt with a beige blouse, plaid suspenders, and scuffed-toed brown shoes. My legs are spread apart like a little boy, and I am holding a tiny doll that is wearing a blue dress and a satin hat just like Scarlett O'Hara's-- my life as a child summed up in one 4 x 5 photograph shot on a Brownie Kodak camera.

I also don't recall playing "dress up" or "house", or "Mommie." Actually, wearing a dress and shoes was something of a displeasure and occurred only upon force from Mama. I much preferred playing football, climbing trees, or running around the track we built in our small backyard that also served as our softball field in the spring. When my brother Jim and I were growing up, I was the only girl in our neighborhood. This fit right into my proclivity for "boy" things. I enjoyed playing "doctor"—not the kind where the girl plays the nurse and the boy plays the doctor or the "I'll show you mine if you show me yours." My doctor version took place in our makeshift operating room cutting off the heads of caterpillars and switching them with other caterpillar heads. Johnson Band-Aids worked great to adhere the heads to the bodies after the delicate surgery. These activities, of course, horrified my mother. This was not what she had in mind when she dreamed all those years ago of dressing up her dainty, petite baby girl. If there was a polar opposite, I was it.

Many times I heard her in tears as she expressed her concern to her family and friends wondering aloud what would become of me. How had God allowed this anomaly to occur? I could not imagine giving up running barefoot, playing football, climbing trees, or jumping in mud puddles in the rain. And yet my greatest desire in life was to please my mother. When I did not, which was often, I suffered. This desperate need to placate was the driving force behind my attempt at being something I was not. This pursuit administered a near fatal blow to my sense of well-being. These were life's questions. There was nothing in my environment that answered them or soothed my angst in any way.

The 1950s Southern lifestyle was dominated by the male figure. Women played a secondary role. They fulfilled their function of servitude to their family in the shadow of their husband without complaints. They dressed appropriately for all occasions, careful to hide the parts of their bodies that were uniquely feminine. Dress lengths fell below the knees, bust lines revealed nothing more than their slender necks, corsets hid the unwanted pounds put on by the most recent birth of a child,

In The Beginning: Mama

and dainty purses filled with compacts of pressed powder and rouge were carefully clutched in their hands. All was perfect in the picture these women presented to their world. Similar to children, they were to be seen rather than heard. As a young tomboy, and with Mama as my model, I found myself surrounded and consumed by this world.

Regardless of her concern over the lack of feminine traits I exhibited, Mama was kind and good. These virtues, however, were often over-shadowed by her deep sense of sadness. If big tears and displays of neurotic behavior were a sign of a great actress, Mother would have been an academy award winner. I came to see that this was her only way to draw attention to, and let the world know the depth of her pain. She used it to manipulate and turn events in her favor. In her lifetime, she was unable to learn that she would have been able to turn these events in her favor by merely asking for what she wanted. I loved her deeply, often needed her more than I wanted, and was unable to express any of the feelings I was experiencing.

Once, as a child, I contracted a bad virus which resulted in a high fever and the usual effects of such maladies. I was sleeping in the bed with Mama. I remember lying far on my side of the bed thinking to myself, "If *she* would just touch me, I would be well." This was not something I could ask for. Rather than confront the humiliation of seeking her help, I very quietly and slowly slid my leg across the smooth percale sheet. I gently and ever so slightly touched the side of her leg with my foot. The next morning I was miraculously healed.

In addition to her other virtues, Mama was a deeply religious woman. As she had mirrored back to me a woman's place in this world, she also mirrored back to me the power, the presence and the need for God in our lives. Just as the male figure dominated the family, the church dominated society as a whole. As though divinely ordered and in perfect alignment with Mama's needs, the center of our Southern life became the church. In our case it was Southern Baptist. Our place of worship functioned as the source of our social life as well as the source of our spiritual indoctrination. Churches held a place of status in the community that added to or detracted from the status of its members. Attending certain churches put a family in with the elites, while attending others placed a family in among the commoners.

Our church was *the* Baptist church located in the heart of downtown Albany. In order to properly fit in, one must observe a rigid dress code. The more elaborate one's outfit, the bigger the hat, the finer the heels and bag, and the more delicate the gloves, the higher one climbed up that great spiritual ladder of success. There was yet another criterion for acceptance into this religious community. How a family arrived at the meeting place of God was carefully observed by those sitting higher up on the rungs. Late model Buicks and Cadillacs were among the most coveted.

If you did not "fit the mold," you knew it. No matter how hard our family tried we were not on the higher rungs of that ladder. This class hierarchy was the dominant force and far outweighed the spiritual teachings that were also offered. God's house became a place of judgment, a place of fear, and a place of confusion. Many Sunday services found me looking down at my worn shoes or handmade dress, wanting to please my mama by wearing it, and wondering how I fit into this strangely uncomfortable world of God's.

I have learned not to use the word "always," however, there is one exception. On Sunday mornings, Mama *always* wore a hat. Hers were not from the finest department stores as were those worn by the ladies of the upper rungs. Mama had her own unique, creative way of appearing stylish on a lower rung budget. I remember her following the local newspaper searching for sales in the women's department of those fine downtown stores. At the same time, she saved her pennies in a sock that she kept in a glass jar hidden away in her chest of drawers. On the day of the sale, she awakened early and slipped out of the house to be the first to arrive at the store. There she would purchase one perfect hat.

Her next stop was the local fabric shop where she picked out an array of beautifully colored ribbons, along with spring, winter, and fall plastic fruits, and flowers to line the brim. Suddenly one hat became

In The Beginning: Mama

five. When the doors of the church opened and Miss Flora walked through, she had climbed a few more steps on that First Baptist Church ladder of success. Thinking back, I believe these moments were her happiest and gave her the greatest sense of pride. The means nor the method of how she got there mattered not to her. These moments allowed her to feel beautiful, if ever so briefly, appreciated and oddly safe. It was worth it.

I admired my mother's beauty and appreciated her sense of style, yet it only served to widen the schism between us. As a young girl I watched as she dressed, making sure her hat was just right and her purse was filled with all the necessary embellishments a Southern lady needs for an afternoon out. I watched in amazement and wondered what purpose all this effort served. What was so completely natural to her was altogether foreign and unnatural to me. Each of us was unable to accept, understand, or tolerate the other's choices. Blue jeans, bare feet, and beautiful Sunday bonnets. Broken fingernails and white lace gloves. Bruised knees and peach-colored skin. Two worlds very far apart yet bound together like flame to a fire. Inseparable. Unable to remove ourselves from each other, we were trapped in a karmic twist for the duration of our lives together. It was sometimes heaven, sometimes hell.

One wonders how deep a mother's love goes. Is it really unconditional? Are we being loved or are we being controlled? A mother's expectations for her daughter are high and difficult to achieve. When does her life end and ours begin? When do we look at her and see ourselves? As we watch in horror, our lives unfold together and the patterns of similarity emerge. While continuing on our journeys, we begin to see more clearly and to understand more deeply. Yet are we ever able to separate from them? Or do we mold and blend until we actually become them?

I have often wondered if my relationship with Mama was complicated by the fact that I was born on her birthday. According to astrology, the sign for the month of our birth is Gemini symbolized by the Twins. Perhaps we shared some of the same character strengths and weaknesses attributed to Geminis, making it more difficult to communicate with each other. Or perhaps the angst was the result of the mountainous age difference between us. One generational gap is quite enough of a challenge for a mother and a daughter to function within. We were asked to maneuver cohesively within a two-generational gap while sharing polarizing views of the world from the beginning.

It seems my fifth birthday and her forty-seventh was a significant date in Mama's mind. She rented the local Girl Scout hut on the other side of town and decorated it with what else…magnolia blossoms. After all, we were Southern Belles. Mama designed and made matching dresses and matching cakes for us. She then invited everyone we both knew. There is a photograph to commemorate the occasion. She is in her lovely summer cotton dress, and I am in mine. She is standing next to her homemade birthday cake, and I am next to mine. All that separated us was a lovely punch bowl and a six-foot-long table. This picture spoke a thousand words.

The following morning I awoke with a dangerously high fever of 105 degrees. I was rushed to the hospital where I was diagnosed with rheumatic fever and confined to my bed for two months. Two long, hot summer months with no physical activity of any kind. No hide and seek, no softball, no running, and no doodle bugs. I discovered many years later that Mama wrote of this period in my baby book, "Little Jeannie really (underlined three times) changed." I wondered what she meant.

Even with all the rigidity of the Southern Baptist thought and teachings, church folks certainly rallied around families when they experienced difficult times. Many of those First Baptist Church members from all status levels stepped up to support us that summer. Mama's Sunday School class organized a gift program to give me something to look forward to. Each morning I anxiously awaited the time when Mama allowed me to open one of these carefully wrapped

In The Beginning: Mama

treasures. Gifts included boxes of coconut marshmallow candies, coloring books, crayons, Juicy Fruit chewing gum, and flowers. My favorite was a ceramic "Bambi" that held a small bouquet of daisies in an attached tree trunk. Long after the flowers were gone, Bambi held a place of significance for me and still shares a table in my home to this day.

It was a difficult and challenging time for both Mama and me. I do remember her taking care of me and doting over me all summer. She enjoyed the attention from her fellow church sisters, and my illness somehow gave her a deeper mission for her own life. We both survived without too many scars, and I began the first grade.

Albany could not have been more small-town-USA. The two-story red brick elementary school was only a few blocks away. I remember apprehensively walking down Madison Street en route to my first day of school, clutching my mama's hand. I was entering an uncertain world filled with unknowns. For a shy six-year-old, it was a traumatic experience. Mama and I had a conversation on the way, and assurances were extended. After much hesitation on the red brick school steps, Mama finally let go of my hand and I walked into Mrs. Monroe's first grade class. Once inside I felt a certain freedom and my unfounded fears became a distant memory. After that day, my brother Jim and I safely walked each morning, carrying our mama-made blue denim book satchels loaded with number-two yellow pencils, spiral notebooks, and a quarter for our lunch.

Recess was the highlight of our days filled with hopscotch, softball, red rover, and dodge ball. The school yard had metal swings with sturdy chain links hooked to the top of the frame. As we pushed off, seeking to feel the freedom of flight, we left behind deep crevices in the hard Georgia clay.

There was one master game amongst the many, played primarily by the boys and tomboy, me. I can still feel the stick in my hand as I drew a thin circle in the ground, placing my marbles inside and clutching my best cat eye. I then waited to be challenged by an unsuspecting male classmate in a do-or-die game of marbles. A crowd gathered 'round. With enough English on it, the colored glass spun in place and then shot across the circle, knocking out my competitor's best marble—leaving the crowd in awe. Ah, what a life.

Two

THEN THERE WAS LIGHT: DADDY

As my flight continued back home to Tennessee that day, I found it to be calm and uneventful. There was a time in the past when I would have enjoyed a Bloody Mary and one or two glasses of white wine as a means to ease my fear of flying. Such indulgences also served to intensify the beauty of the passing clouds. Unfortunately for me, those days were now prohibitive and a thing of my past. I was simply left with my thoughts, no matter how joyful or how painful they might be. Although Jim and I were in disagreement regarding our granddaddy, we were united in our love and adoration for one man.

Our father was known to both of us as Daddy. As his baby girl, our relationship was without complications. He was handsome with thick black hair graying at the temples. His sense of humor made us laugh, and his clever tricks made us giggle with delight. He could almost always pull a nickel out of a child's ear arousing a squeal and a look of wonderment. As a small child I remember riding horsey on the ankle of his crossed leg. The other children anxiously stood in line waiting for their turn on my daddy's man-made horsey.

He was kind, generous, and gloated with pride when he spoke about my brother, Jim, or me. We had come to him later in his life. I am certain he loved us deeply, yet there may have been a bit of male ego present in his pride. Somehow having a beautiful woman and two small children on his arms reflected out to the world his male prowess and confirmed that he "still had it." To this day I am unable to put into words the great joy, stability, and safety he brought into my life.

He had been married once before. His wife died while she was quite young leaving him with their two small children—one son and a daughter. He raised them by himself without help from any other family members. He was a devoted and honest man.

Daddy often shared his favorite story of riding down the street one spring afternoon in our small town of Albany. As he turned a corner he saw a beautiful woman walking on the sidewalk. His heart stopped and he said to himself, "That woman's gonna be my wife." After a "proper" courtship he did indeed, marry that woman, a woman I came to know as Mama.

In the backyard of our house on Madison Avenue, Daddy built his chicken coops. They were his pride and joy. He hovered over his chicks like a mother hen. This was rather curious to me as I also remember on Sundays after church he would grab one by the throat and ring its neck. As we all watched, it ran in circles around the old pecan tree in our backyard. I learned first-hand the deeper meaning of "running around like a chicken with its head cut off." Mother subsequently took the victim to the kitchen, and it later appeared on the dining room table along with the homegrown field peas, mashed potatoes, butter beans, and hot piping brown gravy over freshly made white rice. Sunday "dinnahs" like this were shared throughout the South back then. Nonetheless, Daddy cared for his hens and his old Banter rooster like they were his children. All visitors to the house got a tour of his chicken coops no matter the time of day or night.

Another of his favorite pastimes was whistling. If we ever needed to know where Daddy was we just took a moment and listened for the sound of his lilting melody coming from the yard or another part of the house. He was indiscriminate in his choice of time or place to indulge in this playful pastime. His melodies ran the gamut from lyrical to haunting to downright bawdy depending on his mood. The chickens he loved so dearly were daily recipients of his sonorous tones as he went about the chores of taking care of his tiny fowl friends. He was a joyful soul and this was his way of expressing his jubilance and bliss. Being in awe of his very existence, I spent my days following him around blowing hot air through my tiny, pursed lips, making no sound, yet feeling proud as a peacock "whistling" with my daddy. In time, he did teach me the proper techniques, and I whistled long before I learned to put words together in any intelligent or cohesive sentence.

Daddy was an insurance salesman, though not a very good one at that. If a client did not have the money for their monthly payment all they had to do was say, "Mr. Hall, I ain't got it this month." Daddy's heart was so susceptible and generous he'd let them ride and take the payment out of his salary. I often traveled with him as he made his rounds to collect. Many of his clients were low-income black families living in what was then politely called "Negro Town." While he did his business with the parents I had the pleasure of playing with the children. We'd run around the yards, barefoot, hiding under the houses, and playing kids' games.

I remember one of the women washed and ironed "white folks'" shirts to support her family. Having no electricity, she placed the solid black cast iron against the hot fireplace giving it the heat needed to press the wrinkles from the shirts. To this day, I have never seen a more beautiful, crisply ironed shirt. I believe her name was Miss Sarah. There were thousands of Miss Sarah's back then, all struggling to make ends meet and feed their families. I think of them often and hope they have found peace.

Those times with my daddy are some of the fondest of my life. The joy and privilege I experienced just being with him has been unmatched. Yet there was a greater lesson in it for me. As a five-year-old, growing up in the South during the 1950s, I had no awareness of the brewing racial tensions as I ran around barefoot in "Negro Town." Daddy made no distinction between the way he treated his white clients and the way he treated his black clients. Because he didn't, I didn't. This lesson has served me all of my life.

As a result of Daddy's business practices, we were often strapped for cash as a family. Nonetheless Daddy made even this financial deficit fun, attaching a sense of adventure to it. He made us wonder, how would it all work out? What could we make happen? How could we have fun doing it? Once, Daddy invited his boss over for dinner. Mama was nervous and worried about the house and the dinner being just perfect. My brother Jim and I went with Daddy to pick up Mr. Owens. We had a shiny light green, two-door, 1949 Studebaker. There was a large, gaping hole in the floor on the passenger side from which we could see the pavement below as we sped along. In the mind of two small children, what could have been more fun? To add to the adventure, there was some uncertainty as to whether the passenger door remained locked at high speeds. Since Mr. Owens sat in the front seat next to the door in question, Jim and I anxiously sat in the back enjoying the ride with a sense of danger. All went well until we made the right hand turn onto our street. Suddenly the door flew open with a sprawling Mr. Owens grabbing the handle for dear life and holding onto his hat. Daddy jokingly yells for Jim and me to stick our feet through the hole in the floorboard to stop the car. We laughed so hard I wet my pants.

Much to the dismay of Mama, Daddy enjoyed a cold beer or a shot of whiskey from time to time. Such indulgences were not allowed inside the home, so Daddy and the other men stood outside by our shiny light green Studebaker and imbibed. In awe of anything he did, I hid in the nearby bushes and listened with delight as he told his jokes and funny stories. I often heard the word "poontang" being bantered about within the conversation. This key word, when used, never failed to get a loud guffaw from all of Daddy's spellbound listeners. At the time, I had no idea of its meaning yet to this day I still find great amusement when I hear that word used in any context.

Daddy was also a heavy smoker, causing Mama to run away in shame at the sight. As a Christian woman, she did not want to be affiliated with anyone who indulged in such despicable behavior. Back in those days such habits were celebrated and encouraged, except by my mama of course. Magazine and billboard ads featured current movie stars engaged in varied vigorous physical activities with a lit cigarette hanging out of their mouths exalting the great benefits of pulling fire into one's lungs. Pall Mall in the solid red package, Chesterfield, and Daddy's favorite, Camels were all the rage. Filters were not part of the culture yet so each puff was straight, undiluted, chemically-altered tobacco. The danger of inhaling hot, unfiltered smoke into one's lungs was not part of the mass consciousness. The slogan, "I'd Walk A Mile For A Camel" weighed prominently on the side of the packaging in great contrast to today's Surgeon General's Warning. Cigarettes were for enjoying and allowing one to relax and release the tensions of life in the 1950s.

The eating habits of my daddy were a source of curiosity and often led to gagging and near nausea. His favorite indulgence was slimy, oily sardines carefully placed onto Nabisco saltine crackers. These culinary delectations were offered up in flat tin cans. Each had a thin perforated line that wound around the top of the oblong can. When turned upside down, a small key attached to the bottom was revealed. A half-inch slot was cut into each key just below the handle. He lifted the key up with his thumbnail and placed the lip of the perforated top into the expectant key slot. Next he carefully rolled the thin metal line around the key, inching along, until the top was completely detached revealing the succulent cuisine. The challenge was to complete this procedure without dripping any of the fishy oil onto a table, a napkin, or a plate. In his eagerness to consume the smelly creatures, he often lifted one up by the tail, dangled it in the air, and dropped it whole into his desirous and unsatisfied open orifice. I looked on with simultaneous horror and delight. After this initial self-pleasure, the remainder of the salty seafood bits found their way to the top of one of those Nabisco Saltine crackers. This was Daddy's interpretation of good gourmet eatin'.

Daddy's favorite excursion into cooking was yet another matter and brought chaos to the kitchen and created havoc in the neighborhood. Perhaps you have heard of the famous Southern dish, chitterlings. During its preparation, Mama left the house and returned only when the last ounce had been either eaten or given away. I have fond memories of Mama throwing her arms in the air and screaming at the thought of this dish occupying any portion of her tidy domestic domain. Webster's dictionary defines this robust cuisine as the small intestine of swine, especially when prepared as food. Daddy brought them home in large tin containers from which he washed them down with the garden hose in the backyard. When cooked the smell of the pigs' lower bowels waived throughout Madison Avenue and into the surrounding neighborhoods prompting the quick exit of our overwrought mama. The proper pronunciation and the only name a true Southerner ever uses in referring to this country fare is chitlins. If you have ever tasted them or smelled them you will understand why.

Daddy had three sisters. The oldest was Aunt Nettie, an elegant and generous true Southern Lady. Although she lived in the small town of Sylvester, Georgia, she had a certain sophistication and charm. She owned and managed the only hotel for miles around the country town. At the same time she served as the Postmaster for the local postal office. These two titles gave her a certain stature that was respected and honored in tiny towns back then.

As a teenager I often spent weekends at her hotel where she threw parties for me. Crisp white cloths draped the tables. Large green magnolia leaves were randomly strewn about. A crystal bowl offered up

Then There Was Light: Daddy

lime punch topped with orange sherbet. Home made chocolate chip cookies and cheese straws served as dinner. Following these refreshments, Aunt Nettie rented the local roller skating rink for a dance. Round and round we skated to the nostalgic sounds of the live organ music. Someone on the loud speaker would announce, "Change partners and reverse." Off we'd go in the opposite direction, often bumping into each other, falling down, getting up, and skating in rhythm to another tune blasting through the Magnavox speakers. I felt quite grownup, special, and cared about. Sharing in these times with Aunt Nettie somehow deepened my connection to Daddy and helped me to feel more a part of his life.

Then there were his twin sisters, Annie and Rolly. Annie was also called Jack for a reason I have never known or understood. They lived on the same street on the same block separated only by one house. Jack rarely took a bath, perhaps not even on Saturday nights. Upon opening the front door of her house one's nostrils were overcome with a musky, stale odor. We often found her sitting in her favorite rocker, adorned in a wrinkled cotton dress, legs spread apart, bottom lip bulging with Peach-flavored snuff, talking 'bout the weather, and passing the time of day with all who entered.

Hidden under the ruffle of Jack's rocker was a Maxwell House coffee can that served as her spittoon for the snuff and on occasion, chewing tobacco. Jack exhibited great secrecy in the use of this coffee can spittoon. She was oblivious to or did not take into account that all visitors saw the obvious stains from her snuff drippings that ran down the front of every dress we ever saw her in. With a closer look, we all observed these same dark snuff drippings that lined the creases of her lips and jawbone. Then there was the matter of the snuff-stained carpet that lay beside her chair as a result of having missed her target. All the visual clues lay pale in comparison to the lingering smell of stale snuff and previously chewed tobacco.

Jack was also quite stingy and known to hide her money in socks throughout the house. No one knew the extent of this habit until her death when fourteen-thousand-dollars was found in her various hiding places in around and through her closets and the mattress of her bed.

Daddy used to get a big kick out of our visits to her house on Sunday afternoons. He would imitate her snuff filled conversations as we drove home in our shiny green Studebaker laughing all the way.

Rolly was equally a quirky character and shared the same stingy nature. Her house reeked of a similar musty, stale odor. The curtains were drawn and windows were locked. The sole circulation was the warm, musky air generated by the old wrought iron rotating Coleman fan that stood perched on the floor blowing up her skirt during the sweltering hot summer months. In the center of her living room a scuffed, water-stained coffee table sat in front of a maroon colored wool sofa. Carefully placed on this table was a crystal clear, depression glass candy jar lightly laced at the top with a matching maroon color. Inside was sugar-filled Tom's hard candy made in their factory right there in downtown Albany. As we entered we were given a glass of water and our choice of the savory candy offering. The thick air and time had melted the pieces together making a bulging, sticky lump of stale sugar. When put into our moist children's mouths, the original solid consistency had now turned to soft, chewy, cavity producing crystals. The warm glass of water served as a welcome release from the sugar barrage and somewhat soothed our over-saturated palates.

These two were part of Daddy's family, although I was certain there had been some kind of mix up at birth. He, however, loved them, always treated them with respect and shared a sense of humor regarding their unusual habits and idiosyncratic behaviors. Daddy was a unique, happy soul. He laughed often, appreciated others, and shared his joy and fun-loving spirit with all who would receive it. I never heard him complain or say a discouraging word about anyone. Nothing got under his skin. If he had worries, no one knew it but him. He was my one love and held a place of reverence in my heart.

I have a picture of the two of us together that exemplifies my feelings for him. We are standing on the front porch of our first house. It

Then There Was Light: Daddy

is Easter Sunday. Mother has gotten me in a dress, a hat, and yes, white gloves. I am holding his hand and looking up at him as though there is nothing else in my world. Within this faded photograph I can still see the depth of the love I felt for him, the safety of his presence, and the joy of his being. I cannot say that I have ever experienced that feeling again in my life. I am grateful to have had it at least this once.

Daddy's children by his first wife were both grown and out of the house when Jim and I were born. His son, named for him, was tall and thin with pitch black curly hair. He was movie star handsome with a personality to match. His daughter, Sophia, was tall and breathtakingly beautiful. When she walked into a room all eyes turned in her direction as she glided across the floor soaking in all the adoration. She captured the heart of a wealthy Yankee from Philadelphia and married him one summer. Right away she began to share her newfound wealth. Having grown up with Daddy she was well aware of his work habits and overextended generosity. She knew our house on Madison Avenue was old and in ill repair. Sophia's groom was so taken by her beauty and Southern charm, she persuaded him, a kind and generous man like our father, to write a check for a down payment on a brand new house for Daddy, Mama, Jim, and me.

We were about to begin another fun adventure with our daddy. The house was way on the other side of town in a new subdivision. Our address was 1308-8th Avenue—sounded like uptown to me. There were three small bedrooms. Jim and I each had our own. Mama and Daddy shared theirs. The bathroom had shiny, new fixtures and a bathtub without legs. The living room was adorned with a large picture window looking out onto the street. The attached dining room had built-in shelves for displaying the good china and crystal used only for Thanksgiving and Christmas.

Both Mama and Daddy were so proud of our new house. Neither of them had ever been the first to live in anything. Mama fantasized about the camellias and azaleas she would plant in the front yard. Daddy planned and dreamed about his pole beans, corn, and tomatoes that would fill his garden in the rear. Jim and I designed the large backyard for football, baseball, running track, and climbing trees. It was a tomboy's dream.

Those enchanting summer nights were made luscious by the twinkling lights of the illusive free-flying lightning bugs that captivated our imaginations. The glass Mason jars Mama used to can her fresh vegetables were the perfect receptacles for capturing these exquisite, ethereal creatures. Daddy punched holes in the top with an old ice pick so they could breathe while in captivity. We watched them for hours as their flickering lights bounced off the glass walls and reflected into the sultry summer nights.

It was a happy time with Daddy. It was a safe time. It was a carefree time. My heart was light and filled with joy. I actually believe I was a child and experienced life through the eyes of a child.

When we were a family.

Daddy and his chickens.

My first bike means freedom.

Me and Scarlett O'Hara.

Easter Sunday on the green Studebaker.

Our new home.

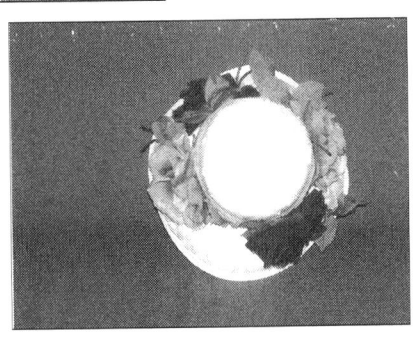

One of Mama's hats.

Three

INTO THE RED SEA: A BAD, WRONG TURN

Jim and I had such fond, happy memories of our daddy. It was hard for me to understand where things had gone awry. As the plane cruised thirty-thousand-feet above the earth, I wondered where the mistrust had begun to creep in. As I thought more deeply, I came across a possible beginning. One that Jim and I could hardly speak of as adults, although it began long ago.

The move to our new house brought with it adventures and challenges. It was a cleaner, newly built neighborhood that brought unfamiliar faces and a state-of-the-art elementary school. We had a little further to go, so rather than walking Jim and I chose to ride our bikes over the dusty unpaved side streets to arrive in class on time. With the piercing sound of the final school bell at the end of the day, we would jump on our Schwinn bikes, strap our book satchels over the handle bars, cut wheelies in the parking lot, and head for home with the wind blowing through our hair. It was a ride of freedom every afternoon. No one feared for our safety.

Into the Red Sea: A Bad, Wrong Turn

On rainy, cold days Mama dropped us off at the school's front door next to the principal's office. Our very strict principal, Miss Powell, lived directly across the street from us, so Jim and I had to be particularly careful. We ran the risk of getting a knock on the door if our neighborhood behavior was not pleasing to her. In addition we had the ongoing pressure of our playground behavior monitored by the unwanted eye of our cross-the-street neighbor. I started the second grade there in Palmyra Elementary and Jim started the fourth.

I began this year in Miss Rachel's class, known to the other students as the "meany" teacher. She was strict, permitted no foolishness, and demanded more from us than some were willing to give. As I look back over the teachers I had during all my educational experiences, Miss Rachel is the one who challenged me the most and assisted me in digging deeper and going further than I believed was possible. I have always been grateful to her for awakening that sense of challenge within my budding, eager mind.

Shortly after we moved into our Eighth Avenue home, Daddy got sick and had to be hospitalized. He was diagnosed with pneumonia and emphysema—neither of which had any meaning to me at the time. I only knew that he was not home to kiss me good night, rock me on his knee, or tell me a funny story.

One night Mama dressed Jim and I for a visit to see him. I was filled with expectancy at the thought of exploring a hospital from the inside for the first time. As we walked down the hallways my youthful eyes fell to each open door. I found myself overcome with curiosity and desire to witness the infirmities of the patients as they lay in their beds. The muted voices from within swelled in my eager ears. The nurses in their crisp white uniforms dashed about with bedpans, medications, and bowls of green and red Jello.

When we reached Daddy's floor, my heart pounded with anticipation of once again seeing his smile, hearing the sound of his voice, and luxuriating in the sweetness of his joyful laughter. The door to his room was partially closed. Mama cracked it further as we peeked in to see him lying there. The upper portion of his body, as well as most of the bed, was covered with a clear plastic hood-like apparatus. It slightly moved in and out with each breath that he took. Large green metal canisters were standing upright next to his bed. Mama told us it was an oxygen tent that would help him breathe better so he could get well. When Daddy saw Jim and I walk into the room, his big brown eyes lit up like diamonds in the black of night. Mama zipped open the side of the tent. I reached my hand inside and rested it against his. His smile was smaller and his laughter softer, but I knew his heart was big as ever.

A few days later my very handsome older brother Clarence, Mama's first born son from her first marriage, arrived at school to pick me up. I did not know he was coming to visit us, so I was excited to see him. He always dressed in the finest of suits and wore interesting, stylish shoes. I was so proud of him. It made me feel good that all my classmates had a chance to see him. I felt special and somehow just his presence set me apart from the others for that one brief moment. He had a conversation with Miss Rachel in the hall and then she called me out of class.

"You are going to leave a little early today," she said as I walked up to her.

"What about my homework for tomorrow?" I asked.

"Let's not give you any. How about that?"

She patted me on my head, and I grabbed my brother's hand. I was excited to have a respite from the grueling second grade class work.

Clarence had a nice new car, and I enjoyed talking to him and taking the short ride to our new house. When we got to our block, I noticed that the street was lined with cars. I remember asking him if we were having a party. The house was filled with people. Clarence took me into the back bedroom that belonged to my brother Jim. The bright spring sun was cascading through the windowpane and bouncing off Mama's cedar chest that held so many of her "precious" treasures. Clarence invited me to sit beside him there.

Into the Red Sea: A Bad, Wrong Turn

"Your daddy has been very sick. He was not getting any better. So he has gone to heaven to be with God," he said with a sweet voice as he took my hand.

Suddenly my tiny body was struck with excruciating pain. My only thoughts were "No, no, no." The beautiful sunlight that only moments before had cascaded into the room, now cast a shadow over my heart. The shiny new hardwood floor began to spin. Breath escaped me. How could my beloved daddy not come home to me? Surely God had made a mistake. How could He need my daddy more than me?

The loss was so profound I was rendered speechless. I said not one word. I recognized in that moment, that love hurt more than I could hold. I simply consciously and completely closed my heart.

As though flying on the wings of some obscure, rare species of bird I found myself in the doorway of my mama's bedroom. The beauty of the April sunlight had been blocked by the closed Venetian blinds. Although it was early afternoon, Mama was already in a nightgown with her hair pulled back off of her face. Sitting on the bed and standing in repose around her was her family and many of her friends. Each in their own way was consoling and attending to her every need. All their saddened eyes drifted toward me as I entered the room. I could see her despair and devastation as she experienced her loss. I could hardly contain all the feelings that were welling up in my tiny, seven-year-old body. I don't recall her reaching out to me, although I am open to the possibility that she did. She appeared to be utterly and completely helpless and overcome with grief. Whatever feelings of loss I was experiencing, I brutally, abruptly and without mercy, assassinated them. I made the decision to save her. I aborted my childhood and turned myself over to Mama.

The doorbell's insistent buzz pierced my hollowness as other well-wishers arrived bringing food and condolences. The house was alive with muffled voices as church folks sipped sweet iced-tea and shared fond memories of my daddy. No one seemed to notice that I was floating out of my body.

I wandered into Jim's room, crawled onto the top bunk bed, and with my back to the door I attempted to disappear into the wall. My secret hiding place was adjacent to the kitchen that was alive with activity. Many of Mama's sisters were putting the food offerings away and making sure that all the guests had what they needed. As they worked I could hear them chatting.

"I don't know how Flora is gonna get through this again. Losing one husband is bad enough, but two."

"And now having to raise the children without a man for a second time. I just don't know how she's gonna do it."

The conversation then turned to my nine-year-old brother, Jim.

"I feel sorry for little Jimmy. It is so hard for a boy to lose his daddy. Now he will not have a man to help him grow up. It's just so sad."

Lastly their thoughts turned to "little Jeannine."

"Oh, she's just too little, she won't even remember this. I don't worry about her."

All agreed that I was too young, would not understand any of it, and therefore would not be impacted by the experience.

The funeral was several days later at our First Baptist Church. Daddy's coffin was covered with beautiful flowers of assorted colors. It smelled like springtime as the pallbearers slowly and reverently shuffled it past Mama, Jim, and me on its way to the front of the sanctuary. We followed it down the aisle to our seats on the first row as Daddy's friends and family bowed their heads in respect to us. Mama was dressed in black and had to lean on the arm of her first born son, Clarence, my handsome brother. After we sat down on the hard wooden pews, a silence came into the room. A deep and heavy stillness pervaded.

The front of the church was covered with flowers from floor to ceiling leaving only a small opening for the preacher and the singer to deliver their messages. Miss Culpepper, the choir director, stood on a small riser to peer through the cascading array of flowers. When she placed her Baptist Hymnal on the pulpit the sound glanced off the hand carved wooden beams overhead and ricocheted to the stained glass windows on either side of the church. Silence fell again as she lifted her voice in praise to the Father and in honor of my daddy.

I come to the Garden alone ... while the dew is still on the roses.
And the voice I hear, whispers in my ear, the Son of God discloses.
And He walks with me and He talks with me
And He tells me I am his own
And the joy we share as we tarry there
None other has ever known.

Her angel voice cut through the air and penetrated my heart. The haunting melody lingered for years.

The church was filled to capacity with family and friends. After the service Mama, Jim, and I followed Daddy out of the sanctuary. As we left, I slowly gazed up at the balcony and saw that it, too, was filled to capacity with Daddy's friends. Their dark-skinned faces were humbly bowed. Their *workin'* hands were folded in prayerful reverence. Their eyes, too, were filled with tears. "Colored folks" were not allowed in "White folks'" churches in the 1950s. An exception had been made for my daddy. The "Coloreds" were allowed to sit in the balcony of the First Baptist Church, but only for that day. They were not permitted inside again until after the Civil Rights Act of 1964.

There was another ceremony in the Crown Hill cemetery where Daddy was laid to rest under the shade of a fragrant old pine tree. The bright spring sun reflected off the shiny lacquered coffin. A young girl's soul doesn't understand how the sun shines on such a broken heart. Mama cried. I comforted her. Thus began our new life together.

Four

JUDAS: THE BETRAYAL

So many memories were rushing through me. All I wanted now was to get off that airplane and get to the safety of my little cottage in Nashville. What was Jim searching for when he asked for evidence? I was certain I had laid out my evidence at length for years. Or was the testimony still in the recesses of my mind and not fully presented to the world?

I reflected back to one of those times when Mama said, "This could be their last birthday (or whatever it was), so we are going to see your grandma and granddaddy. Just get in the car."

With great reluctance, Jim and I found ourselves once again at the old farm with a house full of Mother's sisters and all their children. Perhaps it was that "last Fourth of July" as I remember being quite warm even in my shorts and tee shirt. While running around in the front yard under the sprawling oak tree, Granddaddy came up behind me and grabbed my hand.

Judas: The Betrayal

"Come with me," he simply said.

With no thought, I willingly followed him down the frequently traveled path. I can still recall the sound of the gravel under my tiny feet as we moved further and further away from the crowded house. Granddaddy said nothing more as he and I enjoyed the hot afternoon walking hand in hand. Suddenly, seemingly out of nowhere, Mama appeared.

"Where are you taking her?" she asked in her high-pitched voice while grabbing my other hand.

"Oh, we're just going for a walk," Granddaddy said without hesitation.

Mama hesitated for a moment. I wondered why. And then just as quickly, she dropped my hand to fall alone at my side.

"Don't be long. Bring her right back," she said.

I heard her footsteps in the tiny gravel as she walked away.

Granddaddy and I continued on our journey. I had been down this trail before when playing hide and seek with the other children. At the end of the path was the old barn. It had not been used for years except as a place to store rotting cornhusks that might at some point be fed to the horses. The wood had turned gray from years of rains and hot, smoldering Georgia summers. The door was off its hinges and many of the boards had loosened from the frame. Weeds had overgrown the path blocking the entrance, making it difficult for my small-framed granddaddy to open. When I gazed inside, I could hear rats rustling through the waist-high cornhusks as we intruded upon their dark and musty home. A small grass snake slithered by my foot, quickly disappearing into the maze. The air was stale and damp. Then a quiet fell on that hot afternoon. I heard only the sound of Granddaddy's shallow breath.

Still grasping my hand, he led me into the abyss of that old barn. I stood staring at the squirming, pungent cornhusks. Overcome with emotion, my instinct was to scream and run from the darkness. In the next moment, a more potent voice invaded my mind, "Good girls do what their granddaddy tells them to do." I had learned this lesson in Sunday School. Respect your elders and do what they say. I was a good girl and trusted that my granddaddy would protect me and save me from the impending danger of what lay beneath the rubbish. With that, I stood quiet and still.

Granddaddy dropped to his knees on the ground and motioned for me to do the same. I willingly followed. He gently laid my body onto the bed of writhing debris. He pulled the elastic waistband of my shorts down my legs and slipped them off my ankles, laying them beside me. His yellow tobacco-stained fingers slipped under my panties. He took a quick breath in and then pulled them over my thighs to rest beside my summer shorts. With each touch of his warm, clammy hands, my chest rapidly rose up and down. My obvious anxiety went unnoticed by him. He spread one leg wide, then the other, leaving me open and exposed.

"Shhhhh," he put his index finger over his pursed lips and whispered.

I lay frozen in fear. As Granddaddy rocked on his knees, he quietly unzipped his tattered, gravy-stained pants. With his aging, weather-worn hand, he grabbed his rather large, swollen penis and rubbed it 'round and 'round. Then he took another quick breath in and began to make a low moaning sound. His eyes rolled up into the back of his head as they slowly closed.

"Touch it. Touch it for me," he said as he laid his pounding penis against my quivering thigh.

While staring glassy-eyed at the roof, I spotted a tiny beam of sunlight peeking through as though it was stretching down to rescue me from the damage that was being wielded upon me. I lay motionless and non-responsive. I wondered why my mama had let my hand slip out of hers only a few moments before. Desperate for the answer, I am certain I left my body to the refuge of that tiny beam of sunlight.

I do not know how long it was before I felt Granddaddy's moist lips kissing me on my forehead.

"You are pretty. And you're a good girl, too," he said in a sweet voice as he leaned over me.

With that he stuffed his limp penis away and zipped his pants.

"Remember, this is our little secret. Something we do together, and no one else should know about it," he said.

Granddaddy lifted me off the rat-infested bed, grabbed my hand, and led me back up the path to the house. The tiny gravel on the path now sounded like thunder under my feet. As we grew closer, I could hear loud voices and laughter coming from the living room where my family was gathered. No one had come to help. No one had come to rescue me.

Granddaddy let my hand go just as we got to the front porch. I walked into the house overcome with shame, feeling alone and discarded. I had no idea this was only the beginning.

Evidence.

Five

LIFE A.D.

I arrived safely in Nashville where I was met by friends for the short ride to my cozy cottage among the trees. That night I rested comfortably in my own bed and reflected on my conversation with Jim. As I searched through the crevices of my mind, I was struck by one question. What in my world prevented me from walking into that old farm house that hot afternoon and telling my mother what had happened? Telling anyone? Why didn't I offer up the evidence at the scene of the crime? I pondered further.

As that small child, I did not fully understand what had happened. There was no word in my vocabulary to define it. Shockingly, no one had ever said, "Don't ever let anyone touch your private parts." I did not know not to do it because until that afternoon it was not in my consciousness. I did not know so many things. I did know that it hurt. I did know that it was wrong. No one, no one had to tell me that.

As that long night extended into the early morning, I pondered further why my word was not sufficient evidence for my brother. Our life together had certainly not been easy and much was left unspoken.

Life A.D.

The most significant impact on our lives was the deep sense of loss we both experienced over the death of our daddy. On those rare occasions when we spoke of him, we both welled-up with tears at the mention of his name. As children, we each took on the burden of that loss silently and inwardly. We built our individual castles around our hearts with moats to protect us from the outside world. No one was to be trusted.

At the time, for me, all that mattered was that Daddy died. The safety of his presence, the joy of his laughter, the depth of the love I felt for him reverberated in my memory. The emptiness left behind incarnated as a bomb eager to explode. With no worthy recipient of my innocent and heartfelt adoration, it simply lay pulsating inside. It began to eat me alive. Out of desperation, I made yet another life altering decision. I recognized that love's loss was too great a burden to bear. It required a sacrifice far more challenging than I was willing to pursue. With that recognition, I defused the bomb and threw it as far away from me as my tiny arms could throw it. Love was no longer a part of my awareness nor was it to be spoken of again.

Life went on. None of us spoke of our loss. Jim and I each carried our pain silently and exhibited it in very different ways. Mama was vocal and unashamed of expressing her sorrow in the most obvious of ways often taking to her bed with grief.

I cannot know the depth of my brother Jim's pain nor what it must have felt like to lose the one stable person in his life. Age nine is a critical time for a young boy. Now he was left with an overly emotional mother and a younger sister that he despised. His hell must have been daunting and quite overwhelming. On top of the usual rebellions of a boy, Jim was being asked to face these years without a father or any male figure to guide him.

I was often on the receiving end of his mounting rage, frequently finding myself held down on my back as he exploded his fists into my fragile body and newly budding breasts. During these times I was deeply frightened to be alone with him, yet on some level I had a dark and sullen understanding of the depth of his pain and anger. Other than these neurotic, explosive encounters, Jim and I avoided each other by spinning quietly in our parallel universes of hurt and loss.

In retrospect, it is now much easier to recognize my mama's courage. She, for the second time in her life, had to figure out how as a single woman to raise her two small children. She was equipped with a high school diploma and only the skills of most mothers in the 1950s—housekeeping, cooking, taking care of a husband, and all that raising children entailed. Although these skills were invaluable at the time, there was no job market to accommodate these services. No salary cap. No glass ceiling to try to break through. No career opportunities other than the position affectionately called a "wife and mother." One simple phrase described a life of devotion, selflessness, compassion, and powerlessness—a "wife and mother." Often used as though it had no real value in the world and yet it held all of life in it.

I never learned her process or how she elicited from her situation a conclusion that would solve her immediate needs. I suspect she knelt in prayer many nights alone in her room until she found her very logical solution. She went back to school and became a certified dietician, a cook—a position for which she was highly qualified with multiple years of experience.

Her first job was working in the cafeteria of the Isabella Elementary School as the head cook way on the other side of town. This was not a job for sissies. Her frail frame lifted heavy pots of canned beans and potatoes onto the industrial-size stoves as steam billowed up onto her pale drawn face. I wonder now what thoughts drifted through her mind as she dutifully performed the required tasks. One day her life was complete with a husband and two small children. In a matter of moments the safety of that life had been transformed into a life vacant of the amenities that she had once loved and enjoyed. She now swallowed her pride, bit her lower lip, and drove the fifteen miles to work each morning. It was a most challenging, unappreciated, and thankless job. It paid her mortgage and allowed her to bring home left over food at the end of each day. This helped to keep her children fed and healthy. She did what she had to do.

The humiliation of having Mama work in the school cafeteria was a source of great embarrassment for this young girl. None of my friends' mothers needed to work outside of the home and certainly not as a cook. My humiliation is matched only by the shame I experience in looking back at the selfishness of my childish thoughts and behaviors. Her guts and her great sense of pride cause me to weep when reflecting on her silently standing in that hot, smoldering kitchen, sweat dripping from her brow, struggling to lift those pots or shuck those corn husks, all in an effort to feed her fatherless children. Contrast this with the stunning vision of her walking up those marble steps to the First Baptist Church, head held high, donning one of her homemade, specially-designed sale hats looking for all the world like a woman of great wealth and dignity. That was Mama's life. One filled with contradictions and polarities. As an unknown consequence, this life became mine. I wish I could have seen then what I see now. Yet as adults we must forgive ourselves for our thoughtless actions perpetrated against others while in our self-absorbed childhood years.

Mama was lonely and seemed to be the saddest after the sun set in the evenings. It hurt my heart to see her so forlorn and bewildered. Although I had my own room in our new house, one night I left its safety, crossed the tiny hallway to Mama's room, and crawled into her bed to comfort her. She turned back the cotton percale sheets to welcome me and symbolically tightened the noose that I had stepped into. I stayed there until I went away to college at age seventeen, sleeping every night with her, in an impotent attempt to fill the vacancy left in her heart by the loss of her husband and my daddy.

As time passed and we each began to heal our wounds, now and again we shared a laugh. In those rare times Mama's face lit up like a full moon in the heat of summer and her eyes twinkled like stars in the Southern sky. Her sweet, enchanting, contagious laughter filled the air with calmness and serenity. My heart soared and my spirits lifted far beyond the rooftops of our quaint, homespun neighborhood. These moments gave me hope that one day my happy and content mama would return.

Our tiny kitchen was barely large enough to hold the stove and refrigerator. We somehow were able to fit in a small black and white enamel table where we ate most of our meals. Often during the cold winter months, Mama would make oyster stew in the evening. Neither crab nor halibut were within her budget, however, oysters were affordable and could be picked up at the local fish market on her way home from work. I can remember the steam escaping from the pot and drifting through the slightly opened back door as the chill of the night wafted in. The glass windowpanes, dripping with the crisp winter moisture, became the pallet upon which we marked our initials for a temporary immortality. Oysters were not high on my list of perfect food choices, however, it was the cream and the melted butter that drifted to the top of the bowl that tantalized my taste buds. The plethora of palate delights was completed by the crumbled oyster crackers that floated and then sank to the bottom oozing with the creamy, buttery decadence. The oysters themselves always remained in the bottom of the bowl at the end of the scrumptious meal. Mama would finish them off as she cleaned the table.

Many other delights were brought into our lives by our big sister, Sophia, the one who married the Yankee and moved up North. Mama received a call that she was coming to visit and would be bringing a surprise. Jim and I awaited her arrival with great expectation and excitement. On the appointed day, we drove to the airport with Mama to meet her plane. The one-runway Albany airport lay silent as we watched the skies with anticipation. The minutes were weighted with impatience. Finally a dot appeared above the distant horizon. As it grew larger, the sound of the single engine Bonanza plane came within our hearing range. I could hardly hold my feet on the ground as I watched it circle and make its final approach to the runway. Abruptly the tiny plane landed with a bounce. I could see my sister's beautiful smile through the window as she waved to me, Jim, and Mama.

The door to the Bonanza opened and out bounced our six-foot-tall Sophia. We dashed across the runway to meet her. Let it be noted that in our world today we might be taken into custody for "dashing across the runway" to meet her. However, it was a much simpler life in Small-Town-America that summer day. As we approached her, she leaned down to give us each a kiss. Her bright red lipstick left a sweet mark on our cheeks.

As we waited for her luggage, a tall figure emerged from the plane. Sophia introduced her as her friend, Marie, the pilot. *The Pilot*. I was awestruck by this unconventional sight of a lady pilot. I had never heard of such a thing, and now here I was shaking hands with one who flew my big sister from Philadelphia, Pennsylvania. It was a momentous occasion for a little girl who had longing in her heart.

Under Sophia's arm was a box that we instinctively knew carried the object of our long awaited yearning. Suddenly the top opened and the tiny furry head of a German Shepherd puppy popped out. We squealed with joy as she made her appearance into our lives. We instantly named her Bonnie after the Bonanza plane that had traveled so many miles to safely bring her to her new home in Albany, Georgia. We had found ourselves a Yankee dog. She was to become a loving and caring part of our Southern family until Jim and I both were in college.

The delight of my sister Sophia's visit soon faded, as once again our little family made our sojourns to the small farming town to visit our grandparents. On one of these occasions, for a reason I do not recall, I was left at their house for a day or so. When the visit was over, Granddaddy drove me home in his faded blue Chevrolet. Halfway between their house and ours, he stopped at the general store on the deserted two lane highway. He pulled the car way past the store and parked it on the dirt road. He turned to me as I sat staring out the window of the front passenger seat. I had a feeling I knew what was coming. He gently dragged my legs onto the seat toward him and pulled down my cotton panties to my ankles. He stuck his fingers in my vagina as he rubbed his penis inside his trousers.

"You like that, don't you?" he asked.

I bit my lip and cried so softly he could not hear.

After a short time, he unzipped those trousers, exposing his throbbing genital and attempted to push it inside my contracted, tiny opening. He lowered my head and we disappeared onto the cushioned front seat of that old faded blue Chevrolet.

Lying on my back, I glared out the front window. I could still see the gray Spanish moss loosely hanging from the old oak trees and swaying with the gentle breeze of the summer day. The trees that lined the creek where Jim and I played had the same Spanish moss. It looked so different that day.

A soft rain hit the windshield and the smell of fresh moisture on the dusty dirt road filled my nostrils. When he was finished, he left the car and slowly walked into the general store. When he returned, he offered me an RC cola and a Moon Pie, at that time my favorite. A small payment for services rendered. He quietly drove us home. I sipped my slightly chilled soda. It was the last Moon Pie I have ever eaten.

Evidence.

We arrived back at our house before Mama got home from work. I retreated to my bedroom to find solace in my music and the safety of my space. The view from my window looked out from the rear of our house into the backyard. It was shaded by a fully matured Cherry Laurel tree. Her out-stretched branches draped downward and brushed against the screened window in the apathy of that summer breeze. Just to the left a Mimosa tree spread its languid wings and offered it's fanned pastel pink blossoms in reverence to all that is good and sacred in life. In the evenings as the sun set, she folded her leaves in prayer only to awaken in the morning, with arms wide open, looking for a new day. I am certain something holy and divine lived within those fanned blossoms. Our sweet German Shepherd Bonnie understood this divinity and frequently fell asleep resting in the softness of her welcoming shade. That afternoon, I faded in and out of sleep and enjoyed the breeze flowing through my bedroom window.

The landscape was completed with a row of Cherry Laurel bushes horizontally lining the yard from left to right. These marked the clear delineation for our neighborhood "sports arena." The tiny remaining space served as our softball, football and track fields. We had high jumps, a pitcher's mound, three bases, home plate, two goals and an alley that acted as the outfield homerun, grand slam, "get-it-over-and-you-win" fence. All provided a sense of fun, playfulness, and contentment. Yet at the same time they equally deepened the fracture between Mama and me as we battled over the role of a young girl in Southern society. Running, jumping, screaming as I ran the length of the football field or in some other way challenged myself physically provided the opportunity for me to feel my body. This became the outlet for releasing the enormous stress and shame of the sexual abuse perpetrated upon me by her father.

Being the only girl in the neighborhood also made for challenging days and at the same time seriously assisted me in learning how to stand up for myself. During those days the boys taught me the rules of my favorite sports. I learned them and then beat most of them at those same games. I fell out of a tree onto my back knocking the breath out of myself. I scraped every inch of both knees sliding into home plate. I sprained both my right and left ankles, skinned both elbows, and stubbed all ten toes at one time or another. I was indeed a legitimate, incomparable, and proud of it, tomboy. Despite all of this, life with Mama continued as I entwined my life more and more with hers finding it difficult to know where mine began and hers ended.

I had a small circle of girl friends. We often went to the movies together or played in backyards on Saturdays. One Friday night while lying on the floor between twin beds at a sleepover, I kissed my friend "S" on the lips, more than once. Waves of air and lightheadedness swept through me. The room began to slowly move as though I was riding a painted pony on a carousel while the haunting calliope music played in the distance. If I had known about LSD then, I might have thought I was experiencing an amazing drug related trip. However, even without that knowledge, I knew I was definitely traveling on a newly found fantasy ride. "S" liked it too but was more concerned about her mother finding us on the floor locked in our compromised embrace than she was about continuing our escapade. I experienced a bit of humiliation yet mostly a sense of curiosity about what might have happened had we continued. We stopped having sleepovers and never spoke of it again.

Music filled our tiny home as Mama lovingly tickled the ivories of her prized spinet piano tucked away in the living room. Her sheet music collection of American standards was extensive, and she knew the lyrics to all the classics. I fondly remember her following the melody with her fingers as she gracefully moved along the keys until she hit that one sour note. This was quickly followed by a number of attempts to find that right note or chord and then off she would go merrily singing and playing as though the previous discordant notes were just part of a Stravinsky-like adaptation of a Copland melody.

Mama's beautiful soprano voice found her most Sunday mornings in a long black choir robe with the white starched collar, belting out a classic Baptist hymn. More often than not she was given the solo first soprano part. While sitting in the pews on those Sundays awaiting her first note, my nervous stomach churned like a roller coaster at the county fair. What if she sang off key or couldn't get the note out or otherwise embarrassed herself? When that first note finally did appear and resonated out to the tacit congregation, I held my breath until the last solitary note had left her lips. I was unable to rest until all the voices were quieted and the director gave the silent motion for the choir to be seated en masse. The rustle of the freshly ironed robes pressing against the wooden pews was a welcome sound to my apprehensive, co-dependent ears.

Life A.D.

Mama loved music so much she determined that her daughter was divinely ordered to pursue its joys as well. This meant for me immediate enrollment in private piano lessons with gray-haired Mrs. Smith. I dutifully attended classes for some time, however, when it came to choosing between practicing my lessons or playing football in the backyard, the piano lost every time. Mama stepped in and ordered supervised practice sessions. The familiar sound of flesh pounding against flesh and pigskin swooshing through the air proved too much of a distraction and ultimately turned into pure torture.

During one of our supervised sessions, with great trepidation accompanied by a trembling voice, I announced that I was no longer interested in participating in her tortuous exercises. Her dream for me was shattered. It was the one and only time Mama laid a hand on me. She must have put the energy into that one smack that she had been holding onto from all the other times she had wanted to pop me and didn't. She barehanded me across the face with a force that made my head spin like a top.

"One day you will look back on this moment and regret that you didn't practice like I told you," she said standing with hands on hips, index finger wagging in the contentious air.

I have to honestly say that I do … with all my heart.

Church remained the center of our lives, and like a dutiful child of a strong willed Southern mama I joined the Girls Auxiliary, attended vacation Bible school, journeyed many miles to retreats, confessed of my sins more often than I would have chosen, hid my shame, and got saved. What is it that overtakes a person and directs them to announce to the world that they have indeed found Jesus? It seems to me that this cognition might come in a quiet more serene environment. And yet, one moment I was sitting passively in my pew, and without warning, the music swelled, my heart raced, my body filled with emotion, and I found myself pushing others aside to make that long journey down the sanctuary aisle. All grateful and accepting eyes turned with anticipation and longing to hear my public declaration of faith.

As I neared the front of the church and the awaiting hands of our pastor, my body moved into slow motion. I was suddenly in a romantic comedy and was running along the sandy beach about to be caressed by the longing arms of my newfound lover. By the time I actually made it to the preacher, I was quite overtaken with emotion and unable to speak. My hands trembled and my vision became blurred by the opulence of tears flowing from my eyes. It was an awesome experience and in hindsight, I have to say, a very real one.

Churches have their own distinct modus operandi for consummating their members' declarations of faith. There are as many varied ceremonies, anointments, sprinklings, and offerings as there are denominations. The Southern Baptist tradition of full submergence is by far the most fear-inducing and threatening of all the formalities. Now in full view of the congregation, I was asked to engage in this ritual as a confirmation of my faith. A hand would be carefully placed over my mouth and nose while a relatively unknown man would completely and unabashedly submerge my body into a pool of cool water. It would be lit from the bottom like a swimming pool at the Summer Olympics. All was to be done with grace and ease. No choking, no coughing, and no water backtracking up one's nose was permitted. This was quite a scary undertaking for a nine-year-old.

One of Daddy's cousins, we called "Uncle" James, was a Baptist minister in Florida. When he learned that I had taken Jesus as my Lord and Savior, he offered to fly up and conduct the ceremony for me. Our preacher gave us permission, and the final arrangements were made. On the Saturday before the consummation service, I met with Uncle James to discuss my faith and the plans for the following day. He carefully explained the procedures and attempted to allay my fears.

Sunday morning arrived and as I waited barefoot on the steps of the pool, unseen by the congregation, I was filled with anticipation. All eyes fell upon Uncle James, dressed in a long white choir robe. He stepped into the dramatically lit pool and raised his hand to the Lord above in prayer. The long flowing sleeves of his white robe sank quietly into the awaiting water and dripped softly into the pool as he motioned for me to step forward. Shivering from the cool and dampness, I walked into his arms. As he placed me strategically and perfectly in front of him, he again raised his hand to God. Calmness fell over me. Uncle James gently covered my mouth and laid me under the water. In a brief moment I was standing tall again as he guided me out of the pool and onto solid ground. Mama cried tears of joy.

As a reward for, or in honor of turning my life over to God and His Son Jesus Christ, Mama took Jim and me to Mrs. Powell's boarding house for Sunday dinner. In the proper Southern dialect, 'ers" at the end of words are dropped and are replaced by "ahs." Dinner becomes "Dinnah." The other peculiarity to Southern life is that "Dinnah" is the noon meal. "Suppah" is the evening meal and generally served anytime after five o'clock. So you can see that we were having "Dinnah" that day for our celebration.

Everyone in town knew about Mrs. Powell's, so we often had to wait in line for a table. The floors were made of old hardwood and creaked as we walked across them. The tenants who lived in the house were often single men. I was relatively certain that more often than not they had been drinkin' on a Sunday. At best they had enjoyed a lively Saturday night at the local honky tonk.

The quintessential Southern dishes of fried chicken, rice and gravy, homemade biscuits, fresh field peas, lima beans, and yes, sweet iced tea were served family style at each table in the dilapidated and somewhat seedy dining room. Dessert every Sunday was strawberry shortcake topped with freshly whipped cream—cream that was actually hand-whipped with a fork rather than squirted from a can—can you imagine? Total price for a family of three was one dollar and fifty cents.

Soon after my submergence ceremony, a dark cloud of contentiousness began to form over our beloved First Baptist Church. My mama never quite got over the humiliation of the awkward and un-Christ-like experience that was to come.

Some of the open-minded, compassionate and wise elders had

surmised that our preacher's services were no longer useful and it was time for him to find another spiritual home. Many of the members who had helped build the church with Dr. Stevens were pleased with him and wanted him to stay and continue God's work with us. A collision of egos, rightness and wrongness, finger pointing, questions of faith, and dirty politics took hold of our congregation. The governing body of the church, the board of deacons, comprised only of white middle-aged men, made a decision. In order to resolve their issues, the church members must vote for or against the preacher.

With this decision, the board announced that two ten-gallon aluminum trash cans would be placed in the front of the sanctuary. One was marked with a large black, "Yes." The other with a large black, "No." A "Yes" vote would permit him to continue his life's work. A "No" vote meant immediate termination. All of this shameful arrogance was to be displayed in the presence and in full view of the embattled preacher. While Dr. Stevens, the board of deacons and the entire congregation watched, each faithful servant of the Lord was to walk down the aisle in single file, drop their hand written note into their chosen trash can, and quietly return to their pew where they sat next to their neighbors and life long friends. Mama suffered greatly over her decision and even more deeply of having to openly expose her most intimate of choices. At the end of the evening, the votes were tallied. Our beloved Dr. Stevens, dressed in a white linen suit, was asked to leave the church he had so diligently served for twenty-years.

Shortly thereafter, we moved to a small church that was beginning to grow and spread its wings into our charming, suburban neighborhood. The pastor was a chunky young man with dark black hair and a booming happy voice. As a family, we got right into new activities and doing our part to build a new house for God. I think this helped soothe Mama's wounded heart and gave her a sense of hope again about her faith.

As our three-pronged family made its way through our separate yet coexisting lives, I became more and more aware of the oddity of our configuration in the surrounding culture. Most families were headed by a father and then quietly supported by the submissive wife and dutiful children. We felt more like a tricycle with a broken wheel running in a continuous circle of chaos. Sometimes it was Jim releasing wild spurts of rage. Sometimes it was Mama exposing her bouts of depression and tearful outbursts of pain. Many times it was me, so confused and filled with shame and despair, that I am certain I was insufferable to any and all who crossed my path. I steadfastly aligned my loyalties to Mama and left my struggling brother Jim to fend for himself.

With these thoughts & experiences churning in my brain, I sat up in my bed with a start. The Tennessee sun was now rising, the morning doves were cooing outside my window and my kitty jumped up for a snuggle. It was painful to recognize that as Little Jeannine, I had one mission in life and only one. I was to protect and care for my mama. At that time, little Jimmy had no place in this world. Clearly I could now see that the seed of mistrust that he had expressed to me in the airport may have been planted in this mama-and-daughter pairing the two of us had created. With this fresh in my mind, I made a cup of strong Kona coffee, walked out onto my deck, and laid back in my recliner to share the morning with the scampering squirrels and flittering hummingbirds. I needed a day of rest.

Six

LIFE CONTINUES A.D.

The feelings I had regarding my conversation with Jim were now turning from shock to hurt. Although Jim and I had not been close after Daddy's death, we had shared some unique and often challenging experiences together. Secrets were revealed. There was a foundation of unrivaled familiarity upon which a relationship had been built. Rocky though it may have been, at times adversity had proven bonding. I reflected back on more of our life together growing up in a culture that was thoroughly Southern and exclusive to the times.

In these early years, there was no talk of a minimum wage. There were no opportunities for women to advance in the workplace. Truth being told, women were simply not welcome in the workplace. This was the environment in which Mama struggled to do her best, on her meager salary, to provide us with equal advantages to those enjoyed by our friends and classmates.

Life Continues A.D.

Word had been going around that there was this new electronic device that not only made sound but also had pictures of people. You could actually see a movie with real actors in the box. One day when I got home from school, there in our living room was one of those high-tech, state-of-the-art boxes. It was called a television set. I did not bother to ask how it got there or how Mama paid for it. Did she take out a loan from the bank? Did she borrow from a friend? Buy it on credit? Back then, this did not mean sliding a Visa or Mastercard through a computerized machine. This was a personal commitment between two people, the owner of the electronics store and my mama. He, I say "he" because a "she" would not have been an owner of a store in my hometown during those days. He would have to trust Mama enough to give her the television set today and know that she would pay it off in time. The store owner's secretary would keep an accounting of Mama's monthly payments until she had paid for it in full.

The details mattered not to me. What mattered was that ours was a light brown mahogany console with a small black and white circular screen. Roy Rogers was galloping on his horse Trigger, accompanied by his longhaired, bearded sidekick, Gabby Hayes. I was mesmerized. A fantasy box that could lift my imaginings to greater heights of escapism than I could ever have dreamed.

Television became a part of our family and perhaps in some ways added that fourth wheel or at least propped up the other three. Mama, Jim, and I shared many fun nights together staring at that circular black and white screen. Saturday nights are particularly vivid in my memory. It was time for the Lawrence Welk Show. This was must see TV for our mama. We gathered our electric popcorn maker and headed over to her friend's house for an evening of television music-making.

Mama had carefully trained me in proper popcorn popping, making sure each kernel was delicious and fully popped. The bottom of the aluminum pot was to be filled to the marked line with a full cup of greasy Wesson oil. The kernels of corn were carefully poured from the plastic bag into the awaiting highly saturated, trans fat-filled vegetable oil. We anxiously listened for the familiar sound of the first popped kernel. Then in rapid succession the remaining kernels leapt out of the steaming oil raising the top of the pot as they popped. The aroma of freshly popped corn filled the living room just as the beginning strands of the bubbling champagne music floated out from the television. It was "wunerful, wunerful." All was right with the world for those joyful times sitting on the floor and enjoying life with Lawrence Welk and my mama. Even now late at night when experiencing insomnia, with remote control in hand, I can often find reruns of those old shows. I find myself right back on that floor, and I am certain that the smell of freshly popped corn is floating in from the kitchen.

Television provided another welcome distraction for Mama's life. The First Baptist Church was not her only connection to God nor the singular solace for her loneliness and despair. A televised Billy Graham Revival service often found her glued to our black and white TV set on a Friday night. From start to finish she hung on his every word. I frequently noticed that the volume automatically increased during those parts of the sermon that she thought might be particularly beneficial for me. Her subtext offered no room for nuance. Remote controls were a fixture of the future and not present for our Billy Graham sermons. The only way to change the volume was to actually get out of one's chair, walk to the front of the TV and turn the knob, something that is almost unthinkable in today's world. I have, therefore, declared these volume increases to be Divinely inspired and a testament to her faith.

In the end, the honorable Reverend asked his listeners to touch the television screen and call God into their hearts. Mama's tired, worn hands always reached out as the light flickered off her tear-filled face. The congregants sweetly and softly sang:

Life Continues A.D.

Just As I Am, without one plea,
but that thy blood was shed for me,
and that thou bidst me come to thee,
O Lamb of God, I come, I come.

The beautiful melody and intoxicating lyrics took hold of the hearts of all listeners present in the stadium or out there in TV Land like me and Mama. Hundreds briskly walked down the crowded aisles to profess their love and dedication to a new life with God. Moved by her holy experience, Mama reached for her purse, pulled out her dollar bill and placed it in the tiny, white envelope provided by the worldwide Billy Graham Ministry. I have been grateful all my life to Reverend Graham for lifting some of the burden off her heavy heart during those Friday night telecasts, thereby relieving some of my pressure.

As I grew in age and awareness, the dynamics between Mama and me became even more complicated and entangled. No one on the outside had a glimpse and yet it was enormously troubling inside my own mind. My goal continued to be to please her, comfort her, ease her pain, and never under any circumstances displease her or complicate her life. I constantly acquiesced to her needs over my own. Although I was still sleeping with her each night, I wanted so to return to the safety of my own room yet was unwilling to travel the guilt-laden path from her bed to mine.

The intensity of her religious views accompanied by her willingness to suffer as did Christ on the cross further paralyzed my own developing need for choice and individualized thinking. Any seed of free thought that began to burst through the soil of my own mind was immediately aborted as though a sledge hammer had been wielded to crush it. I dared not disturb the peace and tranquility of ignorance.

These religious mores of righteousness and guilt were exhaustively battered against the shame of the perpetual carnal encounters and misuse of innocence by her father. How did rape and molestation fit into Mama's beloved Southern Baptist dogmas and mores? How does a young child allow these two opposing forces, rape and God's love, to coexist, remain sane, and "act as though" life is peaceful and we are blessed? Often on Sundays when urging churchgoers to endure life's sufferings, our preacher reminded us all of Christ's words as he lay dying on the cross, "Father forgive them for they know not what they do." I began to wonder why didn't they know?

There was life outside of the church, and school was an interesting means of spending my time. Recess remained the best part of the day for me. My beloved game of marbles, the high swings, dodge ball, and red rover were eminently more interesting than Mrs. Bartley's civics or geography lessons. The sound of the shrieking voices, the flag flying high while the chains crashed against the metal flagpole, the smell of fresh sweat on young bodies as they chased each other about captured my imagination far more passionately than the recitation of the Presidents of the United States or pointing out exactly where Burma was on the world map.

One day while engaged in the sweet smells and sounds of a friendly game of hopscotch, my rather precocious friend Dottie grabbed me away from the others with the most desperate of news flashes. Huddled near the merry go round, Dottie cupped her hands together in an attempt to ward off any potential stealers of the secret conversation.

"I bet you don't know where babies come from, do you?" she asked in her whisper-voice with an air of childish arrogance.

She asked as though she already knew I did not have the correct answer. I was quite confident I did indeed have the most current information on the subject.

Life Continues A.D.

"Of course I know where babies come from. The white stork brings the baby girl in a pink blanket and the baby boy in a blue blanket," I said.

Dottie was unimpressed and undeterred by my whimsical, childish answer.

"No Silly, babies are made when the daddy sticks his pee-pee inside the Mommie's private part and then the baby grows in her stomach," she said delivering the devastating truth.

"I never heard that before....Who told you that?" I remember asking in disbelief with a shaky voice.

Dottie was confident that her facts were accurate, sighting the old banana in the donut hole example as her proof. Apparently her Mother had quite a vivid imagination and handy visual aids when delivering her discourse on human sexuality to her daughter. Dottie's evidence appeared shockingly credible and devastatingly familiar.

The smell of fresh sweat flooded my tight young body and dripped off my forehead. The sweet Georgia playground began to spin in synchronized motion with my churning fear-filled stomach. My tight, muscular legs quickly leapt across the clay yard. I grabbed and pulled the large wooden door to the school building toward me, and stumbled into the girls' bathroom before falling onto my knees in front of the first open toilet. The contents of my stomach had turned to liquid. It was now thrusting out my body as it made its way into the awaiting white porcelain, freshly-cleaned bowl. I puked until I was simply dry heaving and exhausted. Recess was now over. I returned to class, masked my terror, and resumed the usual antics of passing notes, giggling, and making funny faces behind Mrs. Bartley's back.

While in Mama's bed I lay awake for most of that night. In the stillness, I knew that her gentle touch could heal and quiet my tortured heart yet the fear of revealing my secret was far greater than my need for immediate solace. I often touched my stomach searching for the baby that certainly must be growing there. Months passed with anxious, sleepless nights, words with no voice, questions with no answers, and peace never found. Life went on in our cozy, charming, undisturbed home on Eighth Avenue. A neighborhood like any other. Anywhere, USA.

Amongst all the chaos of our lives, there was one respite, without which I am certain I would not have made it through those years. My brother Clarence, his beautiful wife, Martha, and their two sons, similar in age to Jim and me, were my safety net, my tranquil parachute that never failed to open no matter the severity of the circumstances. They were a family—mommy, daddy, and two carefree boys. I was safe there. Mama was happy. Jim seemed content. We often made hamburgers that Clarence, Jim, and the boys cooked on the grill. Martha and Mama prepared the vanilla custard for fresh Georgia Peach ice cream. We'd take turns sitting on the back stoop, churning the old wooden ice cream maker watching the salted ice melt with each turn of the steel handle. The wind whistled through the pine trees. The swing set in the backyard squeaked as we glided in the breeze and as we hopped on the seesaw. Sweet sounds of loving voices speaking and sharing with one another served as an anchor for my family's wounded hearts.

Mama's other son, Bill, by her first husband was another source of fun and safety for our little family. He and his wife along with their two small children lived in a house on a lake. One summer, Bill taught Jim and me to water-ski. He always found a way to keep us in stitches with his sense of humor. Even Mama got a laugh now and then. When I think of sunlight, I recall these fun-filled summer days.

There were other loving events that made our days lighter and lifted some of the darkness that we felt during those years. Each Christmas season Mama and her dear friend, "Aunt Nina," met for the traditional divinity-making weekend. If for no other reason than my gender, I was invited to join in the holiday happenings. Normally, I

Life Continues A.D.

was not pleased to participate in "girl" activities, however, in this case I happily lent my two very feminine hands to the process. The three of us adorned ourselves with handmade aprons from Aunt Nina's collection and began the long, formidable task. If you have never had homemade Southern divinity, then, honey, let me tell you with a humble heart, you have been deprived. The basic and primary ingredients are pure cane sugar and white corn syrup. In reality this is simply sugar in granular form combined with sugar in a liquid form. Most recipes call for a minimum of four cups, certainly enough to send a sugarholic rocketing into the stratosphere.

There is an art to the making of this confectionary delight and Aunt Nina was considered, by all who knew such things, to be a master. In addition, she was one of the few people who saw Mama's demons before she did and knew how to prevent her from escalating into her downward spiral of depression and negativity. Her ability to lift Mama's spirits was visible. She acted as a protective buffer and served as Mama's earthy though temporary savior giving me a respite from that arduous duty I had chosen for myself.

I was entrusted with the awesome task of using Aunt Nina's paring knife to cut the green and red candied maraschino cherries into bite sized halves. Each was to be carefully placed onto a piece of the divine divinity. For a raging sugar addict this could not have been a more enjoyable assignment. The sticky, gooey residue left on my fingers served as my fix to lift me higher and higher as the holiday cooking process ensued. There was a plethora of double pots occupying all eyes of her stove. In keeping with the season, each was ready to receive the assigned drop of either red or green food coloring. The procedure was further intensified by the use of chopped, freshly harvested Georgia pecans. In "Southern" it is pronounced, PEE-cans, with the accent on the pee, rather than puh-CAHNS—an accent on the "cahns" as most other sections of the country prefer, especially those Yankees.

The artistry lies in the cooking time and the consistency of the melting sugar as the other ingredients are buoyantly folded into the steaming hot pot. If they missed this essential timing obligation, the divinity batch was considered unfit to carry their names and therefore found its way into the kitchen garbage can. If Aunt Nina deemed the batch worthy, Mama began scooping out dainty dollops of the red and green sweet indulgence and dropping them onto the waxed paper that had been previously laid down. I followed along behind placing the carefully cut maraschino cherries on top adding the finishing touch to the holiday ecstasy.

Gift boxes were laid out on the dining room table lined with tissue paper. Each delectable delicacy was carefully placed in the appropriate box and gently wrapped with waxed paper preventing the pieces from brushing up against each other. At the end of the weekend, the sticky kitchen was wiped clean, the boxes were closed, ribbons and holiday gift tags were attached with love and our "girl" activity had come to an end.

Mama and I spent the next few days hand delivering the holiday cheer to the anxiously awaiting yet happy recipients. Sometimes while riding from house to house, we would sing a Christmas Carol and laugh with a carefree sense of fun and well-being. I did notice that the thin red gas needle was getting dangerously close to the big white E on the odometer, yet we continued on our joyful journey. Through these happy rides, Mama taught me that it truly is better to give than to receive—a lesson that had been lost on me while sitting on the hard pews during Sunday services for all those years. Mama's laugh, love, and kindness were this child's greatest teacher and comfort.

One Holiday season the Palmyra Elementary School PTA held their annual fund-raiser, called the Christmas Bazaar, in the cafeteria. The long tables that were designed to take the daily abuse of two-hundred hungry students were now adorned with sparkly white table cloths. Items that had either been discarded, donated, or hand-crafted by one of the moms were placed proudly on display. All sported a handwritten price tag. I carefully roamed the aisles with a watchful eye searching for the perfect Christmas gift for Mama. I had fifty-cents

Life Continues A.D.

and intended to spend it wisely. The lovely knitted sweater that caught my attention was quickly eliminated when I noticed the $5.00 sign attached to its sleeve. Various cooking utensils vied for my cash along with homemade candles, salt and pepper shakers, garden tools, and hot apple cider mix. None were good enough for my mama until finally on the last table I spotted it. There it was on a five-inch riser delicately placed against an aluminum holder as though announcing to all who would listen, "Here is the best gift in the whole wide world."

My heart began to beat in double-time as I clutched my treasure in my hands for a closer look. Its beauty took my breath away. Painted on a wooden plate was the most beautiful red candle in a golden holder surrounded by green holly leaves with touches of red berries to accentuate the holiday colors. Contributing to its beauty was the freshly applied coat of shiny shellac. My spirits took a tumble when I noticed the $1.00 price tag attached to the back. I asked the mom who was collecting the money what the price was hoping that she might give me a different answer. My ploy did not work—the price remained the same.

I left the table and wandered outside to contemplate and formulate a plan. With fresh air I was thinking more clearly and knew exactly what I needed to do. I walked back inside the cafeteria, pulled up a chair next to the table where my treasure was still on display, and sat. I watched for the remaining two-long-and-agonizing-hours of that Holiday Bazaar.

As each new possible buyer passed by, I held my breath or otherwise distracted them with a sweet smile or a kind hello. Five minutes before closing the doors that same mom took out a red pen, crossed out the $1.00 and marked in the sale price of $.25. I jumped out of my chair, pulled one of my quarters out of my pocket, and purchased my shiny, shellacked Christmas plate. She carefully wrapped it in white tissue paper and handed it to me with a sweet smile. After all my efforts, I still had my other quarter carefully tucked away. On my way home, I stopped at the Hillcrest Market and purchased my favorite ice cream bar, a Creamsicle. Each holiday season I unpack Mama's plate, place it on an aluminum stand and share it as part of my seasonal décor. It is truly a testament to the persevering spirit of a little girl and the enduring power of shiny shellac.

Mama continued her efforts at creating a sense of normalcy and stability for me and Jim. She knew nothing was the same without our daddy, yet she made considerable attempts at getting out of her own pain and bringing some fun to our broken lives. One of these happiest times was Friday nights at Slappey Drive at the Drive-In Theater. Just as the sun was about to set, Jim and I would get into our pajamas, Mama would pop some corn, and we'd jump in our 1951 light-blue Ford and head out for a night at the movies. There was no individual price for admission. Payment was strictly by the car load. For some reason which I cannot recall to this day, I often hid on the floor of the backseat as though I was engaged in an international espionage campaign. Perhaps I was simply setting the mood for the evening of make believe and adventure.

As we looked for a vacant slot, Mama dimmed the car lights so as not to disturb those other families already settled into their positions. Once we found our spot, Mama rolled down her window to grab the large metal speaker that hooked onto the glass and hung inside the car. We turned up the volume full force, a volume I might add that had no balancing, no left or right speakers, and no mute button. It was strictly up or down. We always chose up. Soon the sounds of the symphony orchestra blared the MGM theme signaling the start of the movie. At this point Jim and I jockeyed for position. There was inevitably some kicking and pushing, some name calling, and a warning from Mama before we were able to quiet down and settle into our evening.

Our small town open-air drive-in was not what might be called a first-run theater. This limited our movie choices to John Wayne westerns, comedies starring Abbott and Costello, and horror films featuring

Life Continues A.D.

creatures from the black and soggy lagoon. Little did I know then that John Wayne would appear later in my life under completely different circumstances. But for the moment, this was movie making at its best, in my eyes.

No matter the title, half way through, after our popcorn was finished, Jim and I needed a bathroom break and more refreshments preferably in the form of sugar. We leapt out of the car with jammies blowing in the breeze. The concrete building that was our destination served as the projection room, the restrooms, and the concession stand. As I stood in line for a Milky Way, a black cherry Charm lollipop, or a box of Goobers, my body reflected onto the jagged and broken glass top of the candy counter. The smell of freshly popped corn filled our nostrils. I quickly retrieved my sugar delights and returned to the fantasy world of the MGM latest release and the safety of our "surround-sound" theater in the car. Many times I fell asleep before the end of the movie and awoke only to hear Mama's sweet voice announcing, "We're home."

One afternoon I came home from school to find Granddaddy sitting on the couch, legs crossed, reading our local newspaper. His cigarette-stained fingers jumped off the page at me. Mama was still at work and Jim was playing with the boys in the backyard. After so many sexual encounters with him, it had finally just become a part of my life. He no longer found it necessary to say come with me, or let's take a walk. He just took my hand and led me wherever he wanted. I followed believing I had no choice. He led only with his insatiable appetite for power and carnal gratification, a perfect synergy for catastrophic eventualities.

This particular wanton erotic rendezvous was to take place in my own, otherwise safe, bedroom. As I lay on my back looking out the open window, my eyes rested on the cherry laurel branches and her dainty red berries.

"Am I hurting you?" Granddaddy asked for some reason, taking my face in his hands as he pounded me with his elongated penis.

"Yes," I said from my position of powerlessness and vulnerability. Tears welled-up in my eyes as my molester showed concern for me as never before.

Showing no signs of remorse, he continued to satisfy his carnal needs. Perhaps he enjoyed knowing that he had such control over me. Perhaps he was experiencing deeper feelings about what he was engaging in with his own granddaughter.

As I lay on my back, I could hear the voices of Jim and his friends as they played baseball in the backyard. These jovial sounds became a sweet distraction from the unwanted chaos I was experiencing. While staring glassy eyed out onto the baseball field, I was certain I saw my brother Jim look up and into my window. I was certain we had been exposed. I was certain that one day Jim would bare witness to what he had seen or somehow use it against me. My sense of shame was now deeply aligned with the fear of exposure and the enormous weight of deleterious guilt.

My secret was out. Jim said nothing. I said nothing. Evidence.

Life just went on. I made lots of friends and became somewhat of a buffoon. I was often called out by my teachers for talking too much. Once in middle school, then called Junior High, Miss White ordered me to the front of the class. She marked a circle on the dusty blackboard just high enough so that I had to stand on my tippy toes in order to reach it. She instructed me to stick my nose in the circle and remain there until the end of the period. My classmates thought it was quite funny and a perfect distraction from Miss White's English lesson. As a result, this humiliating display of inappropriate discipline became a masterful means of ingratiating myself to them.

Health class provided an unexpected boon to my self-esteem and a relief from the enormous pressure I often felt. On one particular day, the room was abuzz with giggles and muted conversations as the school nurse divided the class by gender and lead us to separate classrooms. We were treated to a black and white film complete with close ups of the male and female genitals along with detailed explanations of their functions. For the first time I learned about the woman's menstruation cycle

Life Continues A.D.

without which one is unable to conceive. All the girls were aghast and deeply disturbed by this impending lifetime cycle of monthly bleeding. For me, however, a profound sense of peace fell over me. I began to breathe freely knowing that this rhythmical monthly orbit had not yet entered my life and for now I was safe.

After realizing I needed a diversion into creativity, I decided to join the band without having any idea what instrument I wanted to play. The band teacher, Mr. Martin, first tried the usual "female" instrument, the flute. It was way too dainty and reserved for a teenaged tomboy. It turned out that the mouthpiece of the trumpet was too small for my lips and the clarinet was much too whimsical and without ample volume. Finally it was decided that the slide trombone was the perfect fit for my large teeth and lips. No girl had ever played this instrument in the history of the band. That made it all the more sublime. I was inordinately inspired by this and diligently practiced daily until I earned the first trombone position, beating out all the boys. I often got to display my skills and prowess during our rousing performances of the great marches. Colonel Bogie March was my favorite and almost always got a standing ovation with my legendary and passionate slide trombone solo part.

I received my first real kiss outside of the band room while leaning up against the clay brick wall. It was quite unexpected and turned out to be the sloppiest and wettest kiss I have ever had. Over time I must say they got much better and a lot more enjoyable, however, you never really forget that very first one. Beyond my surprise kisser, I did have other boyfriends although we mainly wrote notes to each other with queries such as, "Do you love me? Check yes or no."

One morning during the winter months, I awoke with blood in the bottom of my yellow flannel, gray trimmed, pajamas. I quickly made my way into the bathroom where large blackish-red blood clots dropped into the toilet. I was completely unprepared for this event and sat for some time pondering what to do. I suppose I did what most girls do on this very important step into womanhood.

"Mama," I called.

The door quickly opened as though she had been standing outside for months waiting on my call for help.

"I wondered when you would need these," she said with a little lilt in her voice and much glee.

With that her hand reached into the bathroom closet for a hidden box of appropriate paraphernalia. I leaned against the toilet tank so as not to reveal my bewildered face. Wanting only to be alone, I refused any further help from her.

I was now confronted with the task of assembling the proper gear to deal with this impending issue. The thin elastic belt with the two metal hooks on each end was to go around my slim, teenaged hips. Did I step into it or pull it over my head? I opted for the stepping into method standing naked in the bathroom with elastic and metal hanging from my flesh. God, how primitive is that? Next was the matter of the very large cotton napkin, twelve inches long, three inches wide and two inches deep. It appears this rather bulky foreign object was to be hooked onto the elastic band hanging from my hips and worn like a saddle between my tender and rather sensitive legs. Surely this device was designed by a team of male doctors hell-bent on humiliating women and their teenage daughters.

Time was not my friend on that cold winter morning as my brother Jim, Mama, and I all shared the tiny bathroom. I quickly assembled the apparatus as best I could so as not to further annoy brother Jim. In fitting with the style of the time, I wore a very tight herringbone tweed skirt to school that day. As I walked through the halls of Albany Junior High, I was certain my classmates and teachers surmised that I had just completed a ten-mile ride on a very large, double-wide horse. My napkin saddle, with all its dimensions, was protruding through the front of my tight herringbone skirt and my legs were bowed like a Montana cowboy. Several years later I was introduced to tampons, and life with menstruation became a much easier road to travel.

Mama still remained the center of my life and the anchor, however

Life Continues A.D.

unstable it might have been. Despite the confusing signals I was receiving about what love is, what it means and how it is healthily displayed, I continued to deeply care about her. Pleasing Mama, keeping the peace and seeing her smile continued to be my daily goals and my reason for living. She did her best to feed and clothe two demanding teenaged kids. Christmases were slim, birthdays non-memorable, winters rainy and cold, summers hot, humid, and somewhat carefree. Jim and I continued tolerating each other. The three of us tried to enjoy all that small-town living had to offer.

Just like Anywhere, USA, once a year the county fair rolled into town bringing with it all the carnival folks with their mysterious faces and unfamiliar habits. Few events in our small town could match the anticipation or enthusiasm we experienced as we counted the days until its arrival. I never thought to reflect on Mama's income or what it meant to her that her two young children would expect to have their admission promptly and fully paid. What would she have to give up or let go unpaid in order to satisfy our childhood needs?

I remember one year when things must have been particularly challenging financially. I anxiously waited for her arrival home from her job in the kitchen at Palmyra Elementary School. I heard the key in the lock and ran to the front door as she entered. Her eyes told me she knew exactly what I wanted. She reached into her purse and pulled out all that she could and placed it into my expectant, open hands. Her sadness did not go unnoticed. I walked into my room and behind closed doors, I opened my tight fist to reveal two, thin but shiny, Roosevelt dimes. My heart sank. How could I ride all those many Ferris wheels and roller coasters that I had envisioned in my mind for the last two months? The dreams of pink cotton candy, hot dogs with sweet relish, and double scoops of fresh peach ice cream lay dashed in those coins I held in my hands.

Soon I heard the honking horn of my friend's family car. My ride pulled up to take us for our big night out at the county fair. In the late 1950s many homes were heated by floor furnaces. Ours was made by

Coleman and lay under the house with a crisscrossed grate placed flat against the surrounding slickly polished hardwood floors. In my haste as I ran across the grate, one of my shiny, thin Roosevelt dimes slipped out of my clutched fist and fell into the awaiting Coleman furnace as though devoured by a demon. Retrieval was not possible.

As we drove along old Slappey Drive on the way to the fair grounds, I displayed my most gracious fake smile and offered my best strained conversation. My mind was ablaze with thoughts of embarrassment and desperation. When we arrived I excused myself to make a pit stop at the port-a-potties promising to meet the others inside the main gate. Rather than standing in line, I snuck behind the potties and investigated the possibility of finding a way into the fun and frivolity without the embarrassment of full financial disclosure. I saw a break in the wire fence. I knelt down, tucked my head and slipped through, seizing my opportunity without hesitation. I was in, all the while clutching my tiny, thin dime.

The feel of the sawdust under my feet and the pungent smell of the nearby animals eased my anxious mind and brought a sense of calm. The colossal tents were filled to capacity with familiar fowl and farm creatures of all varieties. Chickens, roosters, ducks, rabbits, baby yellow chicks, cows, bulls, and horses. The best of the best sported their blue ribbons along their bridle, leash, or they hung it proudly on their confining, wire cages. The pride of the county was on display.

As we followed the crowds onto the midway, calliope music traveled through the night air from the nearby merry-go-'round. The voices of the carnival barkers teased us with the caveat of witnessing the world's smallest lady, the tallest giant known to man, the snake girl, or the elephant man. It was a cornucopia of enticements. Many opportunities to toss my shiny dime into a fish bowl or an empty plate presented themselves with the promise of taking home a dingy, smelly, yet mammoth stuffed animal. I was strong and refused all tantalizing teases.

The aroma of fried hamburgers with grilled onions soon captivated all of us. We paused to nourish our awaiting palates without any

Life Continues A.D.

thought of its nutritional value. The Southern County Fair cuisine gave no thought to such matters. My eyes first fell upon the hot, melted caramel oozing down the plump sides of a fresh delicious apple. I was then drawn to the greasy, juicy stout hot dog that seemed to be calling my name. All longing to confiscate that shiny dime from my tightly held palms. Suddenly the mood was altered by the sound of my friend's father's resonant voice as he took everyone's order for food. He leaned down to ask what I wanted all the while unknowingly flashing a crisp twenty dollar bill before my eyes. I took a chance that I would remain financially even and offered up my order for that stout dog and creamy caramel apple. I was right. He handed that crisp twenty to the vender, we all got our carnival cuisine and my dime remained in my pocket.

The balance of the evening followed suit. At each ticket booth, I was given the opportunity to participate as my friend's guest and as part of their family night out. The Ferris wheel, the bumper cars, the flying torpedo, and the roller coaster ride all contributed to my grand and breathtaking night at the county fair. As we rode along Slappey Drive on our way home, I put my hand into my side pocket and rubbed my magic, shiny dime. Mama was already in bed when I arrived back at the house. I saw her purse on the coffee table in the living room. I opened her faded wallet and put my shiny, thin Roosevelt dime back in the pouch. She never knew.

No matter the circumstances, weather, finances or personal cost, we continued our sojourns to Grandma and Granddaddy's farm throughout the year. Their house was not a large one, though it was laid out in such a way that it appeared more massive and sprawling than it actually was. Perhaps the eye of a child and her memory colored the aura and ambiance of their home. I do, however, recall quite vividly the back bedroom on the west wing of the house. Two double beds with iron head and footboards pervaded the room. Mama often told me that as a child she and two of her sisters shared one bed in order to accommodate all the siblings. There was a door that opened out onto the yard; however, as I remember, there were no steps leading to the ground. In that door was an embossed glass picture of a lovely lady holding a white dove in her dainty, feminine hands. The floors were wooden yet partially covered with worn linoleum tiles. This room was separated from the rest of the house by Grandma and Granddaddy's bedroom.

One early evening after supper, Granddaddy came to get me. As I was now accustomed, he simply held out his hand, now even more wrinkled from age and the hot Georgia sun. I placed my soft and supple hand into his and followed him into that ill-boding bedroom. I lay back on the bed with my thin legs hanging off the mattress. Even though I knew what was about to come, I never pulled down my own shorts or lifted my own skirt. In an odd manipulative way I was searching for a minute parcel of control or the smallest vestige of dignity to scavenge from my desperate predicament. I lay motionless as he took off my summer shorts and exposed my naked most personal parts all the while moaning and softly whispering in my ear.

That evening as the sun set, its soft rays encircled the lovely lady with the dove, making a golden halo around her torso and inducing the glass to shimmer in the light. I stayed focused on her beauty and the translucency of her face and hands. Over the varied and frequent erotic enunciations initiated by Granddaddy, I could hear the voices of my family and their laughter streaming throughout the house. The awareness that any moment one of them could walk into the room and expose our secret was breathtaking. I never saw Granddaddy exhibit any visible signs of his fear of recognition or divulgence. The sense of peril must have excited him and aroused the thunderous rush of adrenaline one gets when engaging in the dangerous. He was blatant and overt with his actions. As always, that evening, I remained quiet, immobile, and cooperative. Once again, retreating to the beauty of the light as the sun set over the little country town.

Evidence.

Our Yankee Dog, Bonnie.

Grandma at the piano on her 97th birthday.

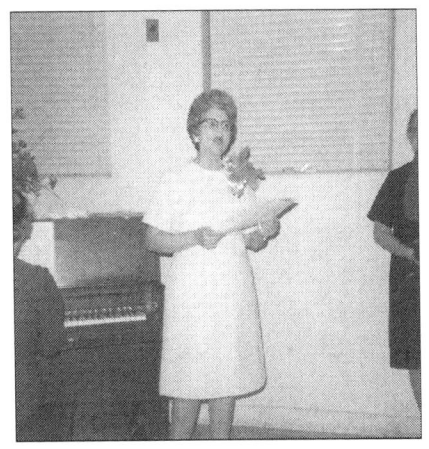

Mama singing at church supper.

Seven

THE DEADLY SERPENT APPEARS

I have to say that I spent most of that first day home watching the various creatures scurrying past my deck. A second pot of coffee was not only wanted but required. Although this was most enjoyable, I cannot say that I was fully present that day. My journey to that moment had been long. My dear doubting brother Jim had played a major role in those travels, and yet he had no awareness that he had even been cast in the part. This next crucial leg of our journey together began during our early teen years. Jim innocently offered me a solution to ease the angst in my life. This solution would later turn into my own nightmare and a living hell.

As Jim and I moved into high school we began to spend our summers with our Yankee sister, Sophia. She had a house in the suburbs of Philadelphia and a summer home at Beach Haven on the Jersey shore. This house was on the ocean with a sand dune for the front yard. We had lunches at the prestigious Yacht Club, went deep sea fishing on

The Deadly Serpent Appears

her husband's boat, rode the salty waves of the Atlantic Ocean daily, and basked in the sun on the sandy beaches.

Blond was in. Light brown was not. What was a girl to do? Thanks to a new hair dyeing product called, Miss Clairol, she could find it in a bottle. Their well-publicized advertising campaign swept the nation, "Does she or doesn't she? Only her hair dresser knows for sure." Miss Clairol could be purchased at any local drug store and applied right in your own bathroom. Like so many other light-brown-haired teenage girls, I became my own "hairdresser." Aided by the bottle and the hot, summer Jersey Shore sun, I instantly and proudly became a bleached blond, almost white headed, bikini wearing hottie.

At the end of our strenuous days lying on the beach, my summer friends and I took a quick, outdoor shower, washed our bottled, blond locks and left them to dry in the heat of the summer night. We then systematically oiled down our bodies with Coppertone Suntan Lotion in an effort to enhance our newly acquired tans. We smelled rather like freshly cracked coconut shells with a hint of pineapple. We were now ready for our night out on the town.

Jim and I, along with our new-found friends, would jump into Sophia's white Lincoln Continental convertible, put the top down, and head for the A&W Root Beer stand on the strip. With the wind blowing through our sun-streaked hair, we drove for hours, back and forth, back and forth, up and down the island. Sophia was always careful to fill the tank of her gas guzzling gorgeous ride before we left.

I have a vivid memory of standing up in the back seat of that white convertible, intoxicated by the night and my youthful arrogance, the wind blowing my beautiful blond hair and screaming to all passersby:

"The best things in life are free
But you can give them to the birds & bees
I need money,
That's what I want..."

A Legacy of Lies

Motown founder Berry Gordy's first Billboard Hit was written and sung by Barrett Strong. What was not to love about a song titled, "Money (That's What I Want)? Motown was already changing what America's teenagers listened to, and I was hooked.

One Friday night Jim and I were invited across the street for some beach party fun. I noticed after a short time that he was outside sitting in Sophia's convertible, with the top down, of course. I walked over to investigate. He had what looked like a plastic cup of orange juice in his hand. He offered me a sip, with the warning that it contained a shot of vodka. I took him up with no hesitation. I found it slightly bitter though not enough to deter me from asking for more. Soon Jim poured me my own drink straight from the Smirnoff half-pint bottle hidden under the front seat.

I remember crossing my legs and attempting to rest my elbow on my knee. It slipped off again and again much to my amusement. My constricted muscles were all beginning to relax. I experienced my first physical effects of alcohol. I liked it. The emotional effects, however, were much more profound. A peace came over me. My angst receded. My mind ceased its racing. My thoughts turned to good. I recall, in the deepest places of my memory, knowing and believing at that moment I had found my solace, my elixir, my resolution to my life's solicitudes. A demon in disguise had finessed its way into my life like the skillful serpent seducing Eve in the Garden of Eden. I too took a bite from the Apple and began my life-long journey with alcohol.

During the next school year, I started drinking more openly and more often. Frequently a group of my friends would load up Claire's Chevrolet Camaro, drive the ten miles to Leesburg, Georgia, where nobody knew us, put down our fake IDs, buy a six-pack-and-a-half of Budweiser beer, and all get smashed riding around town. We had no awareness of DUIs. We had no concern for ourselves or others as we recklessly drove the streets stopping on occasion for the one person who would invariably have to puke out the backseat window.

Toward the end of the evening someone would without exception

The Deadly Serpent Appears

provide the token tearful tirade over the loss of a boyfriend or the shunning from a fellow classmate. The more sober amongst us would assure the broken-hearted that Bob, or Jim, or Roy was certainly nothing more than a dog and the dejected one was much better off without him. Too tired, too drunk, too spent, we usually found ourselves asleep on Claire's bedroom floor in the small cottage her parents had built for her in their backyard. Hangovers didn't seem so bad then. They have a way of growing on you.

Even on the rare nights when I returned home after a riotous evening of drinking those six or eight beers among friends, I'd quietly slither into Mama's bed while holding my breath or breathing only through my nostrils. All efforts were made to avoid close contact with her so as not to arouse any suspicion that alcohol had been consumed. How she could have avoided the aroma of freshly imbibed Budweiser beer is a mystery. Perhaps closer to the truth was Mama's desire to remain in her deep state of denial no matter the cost. I was happy to support her in this aspiration.

Saturday mornings in our small home began to take on a nightmarish atmosphere. Mama, unconcerned about the sleep depravity of her two teenaged children, awoke at the crack of dawn filled with energy and vitality. Out of my own sleep haze I heard the sound of a lilting whistle coming from her puckered lips. I never knew that Daddy had also taught her how to whistle. Next came the much too cheerful, "Good morning sleepyheads. Time to get up." The final blow was the wailing of the Hoover vacuum cleaner piercing the foggy cobwebs of my dormant brain causing me to sit upright in the bed. She continued her cheerful morning greetings over the roaring motor of the Hoover until both Jim and I begrudgingly responded. This is how our respective rooms received their weekly cleanings, with or without our blessings. As my alcohol consumption escalated in quantity and frequency these morning episodes became increasingly more difficult.

My earlier decision to give up my life and protect Mama from her own wounds began to play a deeper role during these years. Her words, primarily based on her religious beliefs, had enormous impact on my thinking.

"Rock 'N Roll is the music of the devil," she would often proclaim in her most high and mighty voice. Or, "Anybody who drinks or dances will go to hell." Or, "Sex outside of marriage is a heinous sin."

In her mind, anyone who participated, no matter how innocently, would experience the raging fires of hell. I was unable to resolve the conflict between her righteous statements and the realities of my life. Rock 'N Roll was already in my blood. I had spent more than one night with Elvis Presley in the "Heartbreak Hotel." I was certain Ray Charles was talking to me when he sang, "I Got A Woman," and Little Richard was calling me "Tutti Frutti" most afternoons.

These new found dance steps came easier and the movements more languid after a couple of Budweiser beers or a little shot of moonshine found in the truck of a friend's car. I was now drinkin' and dancin'. That made me down two and counting in Mama's sin graph.

Her last morality edict was the negligible issue of the disguised-as-normal, ongoing sexual relationship I was engaging in with her father. Her disapproving tone cemented my sensation of guilt and shame. Her words, amassed with my own self-deprecation, made for a most fragile sense of well-being. Excessive amounts of energy were spent in covering up my covert activities and my reprehensible ways of being. Every effort was made to keep Mama's frail demeanor intact. With each cover-up, I became less of myself.

Mama's emotional infirmities and proclivity toward sadness cast the largest shadow over my own germinating psychic structure. I was not equipped to give her guidance. I had no skills to heal her wounds. I was unable to fill the void left by the loss of her husband or any of the other deprivations she had suffered in her life. Again, my deepest desire and longing was to fix it, make it right, make it good, make it

The Deadly Serpent Appears

whole. When I was unable to do so, it became my darkest agony. I loved her painfully. And yet on some level I loathed her even more passionately. She needed a savior. I wanted to be saved. I still remembered that day walking down the path with Granddaddy. Mama came to "save me" and then chose to let my hand go and walk away. For many years of my life, I was tortured by this memory, haunted by its devastating choke around my psychic neck. I frequently allowed myself to be betrayed by this demon in my own heart.

Mama often went into her depressive state that she referred to as the "blues." If I had displeased her in any way, her emotional episode was exacerbated and quickly turned to a darker shade of black. Never knowing the reason why or how severe her status was, I frequently found myself locked out of the house. I could hear her sobs. As the time passed, they grew louder and more excruciating. Then suddenly and without warning, they ceased. There was silence. Had she swallowed pills, did she have a heart attack, had she stabbed herself in the chest, or had she stuck her head in the oven? Those incidents were tormenting and fatiguing to my already fragile and guarded spirit. After she had cried it out or surmised that I had been punished enough for my egregious acts, she opened the front door. The turn of the lock signaled the release of a torrent of tears from my weary eyes. Mama, whom I loved, revered, and could not understand, was alive. My apology and the touch of my hand on hers soothed her heart and the light returned to her face. She had no idea that the touch of her hand on mine did exactly the same for me.

Jim and I continued our abstinence of conversation, careful to avoid any meaningful exchanges. As we both traveled through our high school years, we did share mutual friends. As the younger sister, I could be witnessed only through his peripheral vision, which I suspect was exactly as he wished. One spring morning, however, our paths did cross in the most absurd of ways. While enjoying a quick bath prior to dressing for school, suddenly the door opens and there stands Jim with one of our mutual friends. My naked body is exposed as I grab my breasts and cover my most personal parts. Jim opens the closet, hastily grabs something from the dirty clothes bin and slams the door behind him with a bang. I am left standing unadorned to scream hysterically all of which fell on deaf ears. There was no time to wonder what prompted his sudden and unannounced intrusion. Sadly and with much embarrassment, I was to discover his motives upon arriving to the April Fools' Festivities at Albany High School. There for all to see, flying high upon the flagpole was the object removed from the dirty clothes bin, big man on campus, Jim Hall's little sister's dirty underwear. As my lacey skivvies blew in the spring breeze, the joke of the day was what boy could climb high enough to get into Jeanne Hall's panties.

Later that summer, while visiting my sister Sophia, she took me to see the national tour of the Broadway musical, "Destry Rides Again," at a theatre in Philadelphia. It starred Andy Griffith and Dolores Grey. I was mesmerized by the grandeur and majesty of the theatre—the magnificent red velvet curtain that lined the stage, the hum of the orchestra in the pit as they seated themselves and tuned their instruments, the rumble of the audience, the dimming of the lights as the show was about to begin, the tapping of the conductor's baton on the music stand. My heart swelled with an excitement that almost overtook my senses. This love of the stage and musical theatre would play a large roll later in my life and laid the foundation for my admiration of melody and lyrics.

Music remained a constant source of great pleasure and comfort. I spent many days locked in my room, lying on my bed, with stereo speakers blaring. Ray Charles became a passion. Although he was born in my hometown of Albany, it just wasn't yet politically correct in 1960 for a white girl to be listening to Mr. Ray. I was neither deterred nor intimidated. Ray "knew me." He "got me." His smoky,

The Deadly Serpent Appears

bluesy timbre healed my wounded heart with each note. Ray, my brother, you saved my life more than once.

Already sexually active in the most unethical of ways, I became curious and sought to explore more appropriate means of erotic expression. One afternoon while pursuing this endeavor, Mama interrupted a heated, fully clothed encounter I was engaged in on the living room couch with a young boy whose name escapes me. I do, however, remember in great detail the terror I felt as I heard the key go into the front door lock. We bounded off the couch from our prone positions and greeted her at the opened door with panting breath and clothes askew.

I also fell in love with my dear friend H. She was beautiful, raw, and radiated sensuality. I was intoxicated. We spent many nights sleeping over and enjoying the tenderness of each other's lips and our tight womanish bodies. It was fine to continue our hedonistic trysts after leaving our boyfriends at the front door on Friday nights. It did, however, become apparent that our encounters had no place in our lives in small town US of A.

As I matured and "real" sex became more and more of an issue, I found being alone with a boy, under any circumstances, bordered on terror of epic proportions. After a movie and a quick trip to the local hangout, it was expected that a girl would go "park" with her boyfriend for some kissing, "petting," or more. Being alone with the opposite sex meant being out of control, or perhaps better said, it meant having NO control. The fear levels became so intense, I often contemplated opening the car door and bolting to safety. This phobia, an eventuality and consequence of constant sexual abuse, was something that never got better.

Dating is a part of growing up and socializing in any teenager's life. It became something I felt I had to do so as not to reveal my dark secrets deeply hidden within my daily life. Because of my history with the opposite sex and the trauma created by those experiences, it was not uncommon for me to throw-up the ice cream soda I had just been treated to by my unsuspecting boyfriend. As a result of these secret regurgitations, I lost enormous amounts of weight and appeared frail and gaunt. This became a cause of concern for Mama and subsequently led to a hospital stay to explore the possibilities. The doctors first thought I had leukemia, although that was ruled out after the initial tests. There was ultimately no diagnosis but rather a stern warning from the doctors to eat more fattening foods. Ignorance undoubtedly led to this most uncompassionate admonishing. Of course, it is now clear to me that today the immediate diagnosis would be anorexia.

It was as though I lived in two worlds. The "real" one that I shared with my family and friends, the one that was inhabited by the gregarious, funny, thoughtful me. The other I shared with one man, hidden in the shadows and locked in the prison of abuse and repugnant liaisons with an over zealous and arrogant pedophile. There was no bridge between the two until many years later. As I developed my cognitive skills, I came to recognize the damages and the painful scars that remained and would color my life. In the meantime, I lay unconscious and ignorant to its effects.

The mid-sixties, Southern, deeply Christian lifestyle in which I found myself, cast a veil over all that was real and true. It was a transparent veil of slow moving colors that shaped the picture of my life. No one thought to look behind or even slightly move the cloth away for fear of what might be revealed. Such a courageous motion might thrust a dagger in the heart of those whose eyes want and need to be blinded to the truth.

I recall so vividly the very wealthy women in our small town, riding in their large, audacious automobiles, hair coiffed just perfectly in the same style as the others, smiling their fake smiles, and turning a blind eye to their husbands' infidelities. We all knew that men "misbehave." It was an accepted part of our society. Yet Sunday mornings

The Deadly Serpent Appears

found them all sitting by their wives, dressed in their finest three piece suits with their pot bellies hanging over their belt buckles, reeking of stale cigars, booze, and less than honorable women. Appearances were more important than the truth. Sitting in the wooden pew and claiming to be present, exonerated them from their sins. As long as one sat in that wooden pew on Sunday, one's sins were forgotten.

I was an observer in this veiled society. I understood it. I participated in it as did we all. I hid my secrets as did the wealthy women. I now see that I was one of those who needed to be shielded from the truth in order to survive. So there I stood, in full view, deeply enmeshed in this Southern culture, looking for all the world to be a normal, teenage girl.

Within this world, I learned to carry my fears with me and looked for ways to minimize them. So as to avoid being alone with a boy, I took to organizing "group" dates. One of the "bad boys" that all the girls liked was my date for one of these evenings. Butch was his name. Well, of course, his name was Butch. This "bad boy" drove an old four-door, dark blue Plymouth. It looked like a Dick Tracy car. All the doors opened in such a way that they appeared to wildly swing backwards making it easy to jump in or out of quickly if needed. We pooled our money, purchased two six-packs of beer, and drove out into the country for an evening of fun and teenaged frivolity. After a beer-and-a-half, enough to get us all tipsy, Butch suggested we go to the local witch's house and terrorize her. If you have grown up in the United States, you know there is a local witch in every small town across this country. To six slightly inebriated teenagers, what could have been more exciting? Off we drove down the dirt road to the witch's house, into her yard, circling her house, dragging the clothes off her clothesline and screaming at the top of our lungs. The witch, whom I suspect was not as menacing as we believed, never came out of her house or even acknowledged our nefarious behavior. We finished the six-packs and headed for home.

I had missed my 11:30 curfew, so when we arrived at my house, we quietly opened the back doors of the dark blue Plymouth. Our thinking was that Mama was already in bed so I would quietly sneak in. Butch and I gingerly walked toward the front door, giggling as we went. As we moved closer to the house, believing we were free, much to our surprise out leapt Mama from behind her favorite, red camellia bush, arms whirling in the air, her voice two octaves higher than normal, shooing Butch and all my compatriots out of her yard. The other boys saw what was going on and started the engine of the car. Butch ran back, screaming all the way, and jumped in as the ole Dick Tracy Plymouth sped down Eighth Avenue into the night. I was left with a wailing mama who drug me inside for further scolding and more tears.

I survived Mama's wrath that night, and the "normalcy" of small-town-living continued unabated. An exciting new restaurant, Gargano's, opened up bringing with it an intriguing, tasteful, yet quite unfamiliar cuisine. Foreign and unknown seasonings awakened our palates and introduced our taste buds to new delights. Fried chicken and black-eyed peas gave way to marinara sauces, eggplant parmagiana, and that most fabulous of food fares, the pizza. The lightly browned and rounded crust filled with the sweet tomato sauce topped with three cheeses and sliced pepperoni became all the rage. This new restaurant quickly became the place to see and be seen.

Enjoying a meal at Gargano's was not within the boundaries of Mama's slim family budget thus putting it just outside of my reach. My one hope for enjoying this culinary sensation was to accept an invitation for a Friday night date. With this as a prerequisite, the meal often lost much of its luster as I contemplated what I would have to give up later that night. Would it be a kiss at the door? Would it be a more intimate conversation in a parked car off the roadside? Or would I be asked to leave the safety of the passenger seat and slide closer to the driver signifying some level of affection as we cruised through our small town? The price most frequently was too high to pay.

Although I never mentioned any of these feelings to Mama, at times it felt as though she could read my mind and hear my heart

The Deadly Serpent Appears

even though words were not spoken. Karmic restitution is a mysterious occurrence for sure. It seems Chef Boyardee had gotten wind of this Italian craze and brought the pizza in a box to each and every dinner table in America. The dough, the sauce and the cheese completed the contents of this boxed meal leaving only desired accoutrements to be added at will. Mama purchased a round pizza cooking sheet, pressed out the dough with her wooden roller pin, popped it in the oven and dinner was served to perfection. No kisses had to be given, no unwanted intimate conversations or slides across a car front seat were needed to enjoy. Sometimes it is awesome to see how the universe can bring solace and calm to the soul in distress. Chef Boyardee was one of those for me.

Jim graduated from high school in the summer of 1960. We had tolerated and avoided each other for years. In reality, I don't actually recall having had a meaningful conversation with him at any point during that time. Based on this history, I can't say that I was unhappy about his leaving for Pennsylvania State University to begin his freshman year of college that fall. One night before he was to leave, I came home from a date to find him already waiting in his room to talk to me. This was most certainly a rare event so naturally I was suspicious of his motives. He asked me to join him on the back porch so as not to disturb our mama.

All was dark but for the dazzling end-of-summer moonlight radiating off our faces. His head was hung, his voice shaky, and his stance unsteady. With great uncertainty and a quivering lower lip, Jim informed me that his girlfriend was pregnant. This was not a frequent occurrence in small town USA circa 1960. He had told no one and yet somehow at this crucial moment in his young life, he had chosen to share this privileged information with me. I was stunned, not by the message but by the messenger himself. I distinctly remember Jim grabbing the white post on the porch, wrapping his arms around it, leaning his black head of hair over the railing, and vomiting his stomach contents into Mama's bed of hollyhocks by the back door. I do not know to this day why he chose to share with me that night. It was, however, the beginning of our relationship. As was expected, he married his girlfriend several days later. The ceremony took place in her Presbyterian church, conducted by her pastor. It was attended by her parents, her brother, Mama, and me. Shame had been brought upon her family. It was a sad service for the parents. Jim and his bride seemed happy though. They shortly moved to Penn State. Now there was just me and Mama.

The last couple of years in high school we spent the summer months swimming and lying in the sun on the man-made beaches at Radium Springs. Seventy-thousand-gallons-per-minute of cold spring water flowed into this South Georgia Natural Wonder. Aside from the aquatic marvels of Radium Springs, the other striking feature of this provocative summer hideaway was the beguiling juke box on the outdoor dance pavilion. It was ten-cents a tune or three-for-a-quarter. And yes, there was dancing not only out in the open but in the day time as well. Going straight to hell for sure.

One hot summer day, while idly looking out at the water, Henry F. tapped me on my shoulder and asked me to dance. Henry was gorgeous, a football player and a senior, making him totally intriguing and dangerous at the same time. While the sun glistened off the ripples of the tiny waves and the Spanish moss dangling from the oak trees began to twist in the breeze, the haunting strands of The Platters' singing "Smoke Gets In Your Eyes" began to play from that ole, neon lit juke box. I could hardly catch my breath. My knees weakened and started to buckle beneath me. Their harmonies and the lilting melody captivated my being. I truly danced on air. Was it Henry or was it the Platters that glazed over my eyes that day? Not sure about that, however, Henry would be off to college in the fall and to this day, when I hear that song, I can go right back to Radium Springs, that day, that

The Deadly Serpent Appears

summer, that dance with gorgeous Henry F., football player, senior in high school.

I entered my junior year in the fall. As was the case in most small towns across the South at that time, we grew up with only one white high school and one "Negro" high school. Friday night football was as important to the "Negro" team as it was to the white team, yet we never played a game against each other. We did not compete in debates or challenge each other in spelling bees. Our paths never crossed. Once, during a half-time show for one of those Friday night games, two friends and I left the all-white marching band of Albany High and headed over to the all-Negro Monroe High School marching band looking for an adventure.

The three of us hid among the parked cars so as not to be noticed. In hind sight, how funny and naïve to think that three very white teenaged girls would go unnoticed crouched down on the ground watching an all-black marching band on a Friday night in 1962. Ah, the ingenuousness of youth. I had never seen anything like it. Their drum corps was as large as the soprano section of the Mormon Tabernacle Choir. Their uniforms were multi-colored and every member sported sparkling white gloves. The cadence of that drum corps just flat out tapped my soul. It was rich and powerful. I felt lifted off the ground that night and would have stayed except for the primal fear that was suddenly overtaking my friends. I reluctantly returned to our home football field but have never forgotten the rhythms of my first all-Negro marching band.

I had not yet heard of Dr. Martin Luther King Jr. I was, however, aware that something was rumbling under the surface. I heard the white folks talkin'. New words entered the conversation—words like sit-ins, marching, movements, and protests. I wanted to know more and yet was fearful.

A Legacy of Lies

I began to have more and more concerns about the separateness of the races. None of it made sense to me. I am certain the groundwork for this thinking had been laid by my daddy as I traveled with him into "Negro Town" those many long years before. During these times, Mama still worked as a dietician/cook and managed a staff of Negro women. On rare occasions Mama hired Miss Mary, one of these Negro women, to clean our house. She needed the extra money to help feed her family, and Mama certainly could use the extra help around our house.

Having recently obtained a drivers license I was eager to drive Miss Mary home. Each time as we opened the door to the car, Miss Mary pulled down the front seat to "take her place" in the back. I never consciously thought about it—I just always asked her to ride up front with me. I do, however, remember noticing that she seemed uncomfortable and uneasy as we drove. Was it because I was a young driver and new to handling the roadways? I think not. I now believe that she was uncomfortable riding in the front seat with me because I was white, the boss's daughter, and it was just not done. "Negroes" rode in the back seat. Those were the white folks' rules. I had no idea the impact I was having on her sense of what was appropriate in the 1960s. I did what seemed right and just to me. It is remarkable to think that many in that Southern society loved and deeply cared about these "Negro folks" and yet we required that they ride in the back seat.

As long as I could remember, the department store where Mama bought her "upper rung" hats always had two water fountains. Taped to the wall over one hung a sign in large black letters, "Whites Only." I had used this one all my growing up years and yet never understood why. I suppose I was programmed and like everyone else, I just did it. After I heard about the civil rights movement and Dr. King, I thought more about it and was embolden by the concept of equality for all of us. One day while shopping for the latest, fashionable outfit I walked over to the "Colored Only" water fountain, looked around to make sure no one was watching, lowered my head, and took a drink. It tasted exactly

The Deadly Serpent Appears

the same, as I knew it would. I never again drank from the "White Only" fountain and often discreetly removed the sign only to find it back on the wall at my next shopping trip.

That simple act of drinking out of the same water fountain as the "Negroes" boosted my confidence and gave me a newfound sense of freedom. After leaving the store that day, as I walked across the street, a group of young black boys was walking towards us in the same crosswalk. As one of them reached my right side, I looked at him and he looked at me. We both smiled. Mama had already passed in front of me so she was not witness to this historic episode of racial amelioration. I still remember his face. He knew and I knew we had shared a small yet deeply profound moment. My face turned beet red. My heart raced in fear that perhaps someone had seen a young black boy smiling at a young white girl. Sadly, I knew I would not have to defend my actions. He would.

The rumbling that I felt before had now begun to surface on the news and was deeply felt all around me. It now had a name. It was called The Civil Rights movement, and it was penetrating into the heart of our little town of Albany, Georgia. Members of the Student Non-Violent Coordination Committee (SNCC) started a voter-registration drive chaired by the now famous and well-respected honorable John Lewis. Back then, he was known only as a radical "Negro" who was often beaten and thrown into jail. The Albany Movement, as it became known, started in 1961. It was met with fear and challenges from the white community as well as the more conservative and fearful black community. Its purpose was to desegregate the entire community, the first mass movement of its kind in the modern civil rights era.

Downtown Albany was one square block that housed all the local retail stores and was the center of the Southwest Georgia community for miles around. Right in the heart of the square was the Woolworth's Dime Store on Washington Street. Their "White American" lunch counter was designated as the consummate location for the first sit-in.

The entire downtown square was blocked off and closed to traffic. All willing antagonists were arrested and sent to the county jail. In the early- and mid-sixties, the country's main news source was the national network evening broadcasts. Our local affiliate was NBC. The Albany Woolworth's lunch counter sit-in was the lead story on all these national news programs, sending shock waves through the state of Georgia. I remember many white adults expressing shame that our lovely, quaint Southern town was smeared all over the national news for such an event.

Now I began to hear the name Dr. Martin Luther King, Jr. more frequently. It was often spoken with disdain and out of anger. He was the "uppity Negro who was agitating all the other Negroes in the South." He, along with his followers, were sometimes referred to by the men as "coons." I watched with great concern. Dr. Martin Luther King, Jr., also watched as the Albany Movement took shape. Ultimately he arrived to lend his support. The Old Mt. Zion Church on Whitney Street became a focal point for meetings. I learned on the local news that "white folks" were in danger and we all better take up our guns to protect ourselves. Women were especially warned not to go out alone after dark. Fear was running rampant.

In December of 1961, Dr. King was scheduled to deliver a speech before his local supporters. After he spoke he made a decision to extend his stay and march with the Albany Movement protesters. He led the event and was subsequently put in jail along with Ralph Abernathy. Dr. King and Abernathy ultimately posted bond. They were both released with the commitment from law enforcement that a number of their civil rights requests would be honored. In the end, they were not. During the summer of 1962, the two of them returned to Albany for sentencing. They faced a fine of one-hundred-and-seventy-eight-dollars each. Both chose to refuse the fine and go with the alternative of spending forty-five-days in jail. Before they could complete much of their stay an anonymous, white supporter paid their fines and both were released against their wishes.

The Deadly Serpent Appears

Now I wanted to meet this courageous crusader of freedom. This man who was giving voice to his people or better stated, this man who was helping his people find their own voices. Recalling the faces of many of my daddy's clients and the fun adventures I had playing in their front yards with their children, I felt deep compassion for them. I secretly rooted for them although I dared not speak it aloud. They were finding their voices--I was looking for mine. Dr. King's world and my own did not yet converge.

That same early-summer meant graduation from high school and the completion of one of life's milestones. As previously professed, studying was not one of my strong suits nor was it a concern of mine. As a result, the end of my senior year found me wanting for a passing grade in one of my classes. While my fellow graduates were rehearsing for the Commencement Exercises I was hidden away in a classroom with my very cool biology teacher. With some prodding and gentle nudging from him, I miraculously passed the retake of my final exam. I was cleared for graduation and allowed to join in the festivities—cause for great relief for me and certainly for my concerned and fearful mama.

Following graduation, I planned a trip to visit my sister Sophia to spend some time at her summer home on the Jersey shore. I was to fly from Albany to Atlanta and then on to Philadelphia. I arrived at the designated time to find the airport abuzz with cars screeching to a halt, men jumping out with guns drawn and commands coming from a megaphone inside the building. Three men in suits pushed us back with the tumultuous demand, "Get back. We have a bomb threat." Subsequently I learned that Dr. Martin Luther King Jr. and his wife Coretta were to be on the flight with me to Atlanta. FBI agents and airline personnel searched the plane from stem to stern. Hours passed until the aircraft was finally cleared and we were allowed to board.

I saw the two of them for the first time as they walked up the stairs leading to the plane. Intimidated by their presence, I sheepishly boarded behind them. The heat from the sun and the summer wind had jostled us about. Dr. and Mrs. King seated themselves midway up the aisle just in front of the wings. I cautiously sat two rows behind them on the opposite side of the plane. I could see the back of their heads throughout the flight. I sat in utter terror. My logical mind rested with the assurance that the plane had been cleared and all was safe. My irrational mind was certain the bomb was still hidden under a wing or a piece of luggage or the front landing gear. I knew at any moment we would be blown from the sky, and I would forever be remembered as the girl who died in the plane with Dr. Martin Luther King Jr. and his lovely wife, Coretta.

I have very few regrets in my life. This is one of them. Here was my chance to meet the courageous crusader. Our worlds had finally collided in the oddest of ways. Yet, I spent the hour-long flight in fear rather than conversation with one of the greatest leaders our nation has ever known. I have consoled myself with the thought that it was 1962, it was the Deep South, and as a teenager I had only a few weeks before drunk from the "Colored Only" water fountain and smiled at my very first black boy.

We arrived safely and my hot summer days on the Jersey shore were filled with fun and carefree revelry. Upon my return to Albany that August, I began my preparations to leave for college in the fall.

Right before I was to leave, Granddaddy came to visit one afternoon without Grandma. Mama was at work. Jim was married to his high school sweetheart. We were alone. Granddaddy once again had me for his pleasure. This day he exhibited the height of arrogance and disdain for decency by leading me into Mama's bedroom for our afternoon tryst on her four-poster, ornate, mahogany bed. By now, as he lowered me onto the mattress, my legs essentially touched the hard wood floors below. The chronology of our illicit dalliances could be carefully measured by the length of my legs in relationship to the floor. There are words he spoke that day and ways in which he

The Deadly Serpent Appears

touched me that are still too shameful to articulate even after all these years. Some of these became necessary components to my future sexual satisfaction. Another provoker of great shame and humiliation.

Evidence.

Eight

OUT OF THE WILDERNESS

I was certain Jim had witnessed the crime when he glared into my bedroom window from our backyard all those years before. Now here we stood as adults. Jim, seemingly with no knowledge of the events, is asking for evidence. The misdeeds were so deeply engrained in me that I was certain the world knew of and could attest to them all. I was convinced I had a transmitter on my back that broadcast out to the world, "This slut of a girl is engaging in illicit sexual acts with her grandfather. She could stop it but she likes it too much." My only respite at the time was to dream of my eventual escape into a new world. I vividly recalled those feelings as I searched for the answers that my brother needed.

It was the fall of 1962. I was heading to college and on the way to freedom. The excitement swelled in my body. Nights were restless with anticipation while days were filled with careful preparations. Sheets and towels were cautiously labeled Jeanne Hall with a black marker—my name and no one else's. No more sharing toothpaste with Mama and Jim. No more holey underwear and tattered brassieres. I had my own laundry detergent and a wallet full of quarters. All the amenities that signify independence and self-sufficiency were at my fingertips for the first time. Leaving my habitual, mundane surroundings and heading into a completely unknown abyss was exhilarating and frightening at the same time. There is safety in familiarity even if the familiar is not safe.

My best friends and I knew this was a unique time in our lives, that nothing would ever be the same again, and we would be wise to make the most of it. We did. We partied, we drank, we danced. We swam and laughed and cried up to the last moments that each of us left on our separate life adventures.

Mama and I packed our old blue Ford to the brim with all my worldly possessions. We headed out together to the small town of Rome, Georgia, in the northern part of the state. I would be attending Shorter College, previously a prestigious girls' school. Due to financial difficulties and the changing times of the sixties, it had just recently turned co-ed. This was Mama's choice for me. Her thinking was that I would be safer with a large population of young girls rather than having the usual distractions brought on by a larger number of young men. I was not fooled on any level by this reasoning. I fully understood that her preference for Shorter College was based solely on the fact that it was a Southern Baptist Christian school. My higher education choice was the University of Georgia, at that time a party school where I hoped to get lost in the crowd. You can see who won this battle and why she and I were driving to Rome, Georgia, instead of to the home of the Georgia Bulldogs and my much sought after anonymity.

We drove in silent anticipation with spurts of idle chatter. We both recognized that the chokehold around my neck in some way was about to be loosened. We shared a quiet terror of what that would mean for our relationship and for each of us individually. I knew I was escaping the watchful eye of my mama yet all the while I also was aware that she still very much lived inside me.

After checking in, meeting my roommate and unloading my belongings, the time for goodbye arrived. I was nauseated with fear and light-headed with joy as we hugged each other in the parking lot. We cried, promised to write, and waved our goodbyes. As I turned to walk into my dorm, my heart raced with a sense of freedom and independence. I had long dreamed of this moment. Now here I was living it. It was far greater in reality than in my small, unfeeling and yet unfulfilled fantasy.

Later that evening I made my bed with my newly purchased cotton sheets, said good night to the stranger who shared my room, and laid my head onto my very own soft, quilted pillow. In the dark of the night, I silently cried. How would I live without my mama? At the same time I wondered how high I could fly on my first solo flight of freedom? How could I so desperately miss her and yet be so uplifted by my liberation? Once again the dichotomies of our life together appeared to me as I lay in my bed that night. Although I was unable to resolve these duplicities, I remained hopeful about my new, impending sovereignty.

In these early days, my shyness often got the best of me leaving me feeling isolated and lonely. Soon, however, I made friends with other girls in my dormitory and life became less stressful and more enjoyable. As we shared our hearts late into the morning hours, without our knowledge, we developed concrete *Sistahhoods*, relationships that have lasted a lifetime.

Life at Shorter was entertaining, educational, and alluring. The newly-enrolled male population was primarily from the North, mostly Jersey and New York State Yankee boys. Many were street wise, experienced far beyond most of us Southern girls, and quite edgy for the mid-60s. They were fascinating, fun and dangerous. Most were far too perilous for me to maintain anything other than friendships. This was a certain and safe means of enjoying their gregarious natures without the hazards of a romantic involvement.

Dating, as in high school, remained an infinite problem. The change in my surroundings did little to diminish the fear I harbored toward intimacy on any level and in particular with members of the opposite sex. Alcohol became a resolute and inevitable solution without which I would have been lost. That innocent first vodka and orange juice shared with my brother Jim on the Jersey Shore was paying off with big dividends. I was grateful.

The campus was built at the top of a hill in a "dry," alcohol-free county. My guess is that the founders of the Christian college wanted to keep all us Southern Baptist young folks as far away as possible from the booze and above the dangers of the real world below. Young people told "No," will almost always find a way to make it "Yes." Surrounding counties and states, for that matter, became our supply lines for our favorite libation choices. The Yankee boys were pleased to make these interstate liquor runs, never wanting to keep a sweet Southern Belle thirsty or in want of a cold drink on a hot summer day.

At the bottom of the hill, a neighborhood bar appropriately named Shorter Heights, sat nestled on the side of a main thoroughfare. This seedy old dive became our hangout. The back room housed a *rockin'* jukebox, a tiny dance floor, and tables covered with red and white checkered vinyl table clothes. The neon Schlitz, Pabst Blue Ribbon, and Falstaff beer signs were the only sources of light for the dimly lit room. Most Friday and Saturday nights found us in this slovenly sanctuary playing bridge, drinking iced cold draft Pabst Blue Ribbons and eating hamburgers with greasy French fries. Higher education at its finest.

My newfound autonomy and sense of laissez faire approach to life was exhilarating. College provided just enough rope, permitting me the freedom to roam my new world and yet not enough to hang myself in dangerous and thoughtless actions. Unbeknown to Mama, her world was also about to make a seismic shift. One that would not please her on any level.

As the crisp fall air fell upon the campus high above that small town below, we completed our first three months of advanced studies and headed home for the Christmas holidays. I longed to see Mama, and yet knew that somehow things would be different. As the car pulled up into our driveway, she ran out to greet me. She had on her happy, sweet voice, the one that always melted my heart and made me laugh. When we opened the front door, nothing seemed in its rightful place. The furniture certainly had been rearranged. Surely the smells had been enhanced with new fragrances. The touch of the door handle was no longer cold and unyielding. The air was lighter and less oppressed. Had our tiny, quaint home been an illusion all those years? What was altered? What brought about these meteoric shifts? It didn't take long to recognize and acknowledge the answer. It was me. I was the change I saw. I walked into my bedroom, closed the door, lay down on my bed, and breathed a sigh of utter release. That night for the first time since walking across the hallway into my caregiver's room so long ago, I slept in my own bed, never to return to the warmth and dysfunction of my mama's audacious mahogany four poster bed.

After the holidays, I returned to my new life of freedom and all that college life entails. Studying was no longer enjoyable, so therefore was not engaged in until the night before an exam. "No Doz" and pots of hot coffee were the source of my freshman year scholastic successes. By my sophomore year I was in need of stronger stimuli in order to continue my carefree study habits. A boyfriend introduced me to Uppers, Black Beauties, and Bennies. As instructed, I was to take one pill before hitting the books and another right before entering the classroom the following morning. I was convinced this was far too important an endeavor to pursue without a trial run, so following dinner one evening, I took a single Bennie.

After putting on my madras jacket with my matching madras shorts, shirt, and shoelaces, I headed to the roof of the student building to enjoy the cool of the early evening. Shortly I noticed that the stars were more brightly illuminating the sky. The colors of the night shown richer and more brilliantly than before. The crescent moon seemed to smile down at me with a placid expression of undisturbed tranquility. Although I was aware that it had been falsely induced, my heart matched this expression with a similar sense of pastoral peace.

The significance of my sophomore year was punctuated by the introduction of The Beatles into the sixties pop culture. I recall Mama and I driving through the hills of north Georgia on our way back to Shorter after summer vacation. Suddenly our silence was broken by "I Want To Hold Your Hand" bursting through the airwaves of the radio in our newly acquired blue and white six-year-old Buick. Mama had a difficult time grasping the relevance of these four, long-haired young boys from the UK. The song didn't sound like all that much to her. She did, however, seem to relish in the enthusiasm I was displaying as I expounded their merits and revealed the magnitude and importance of the British Invasion.

There were also monumental events occurring outside my myopic yet stirring life. President John F. Kennedy was assassinated while riding in a motorcade on a Dallas, Texas street with his stunning wife at his side. Our black-and-white televisions endlessly repeated the horror of Jackie climbing onto the trunk of that Lincoln Continental convertible, grasping her husband's shattered skull in her hands. All of America stood still as we collectively watched those unprecedented events unfold.

Three days later, the beauty of a brisk, fall morning was broken as the cortege with its flag-draped wooden sarcophagus rolled along the streets of our nation's capitol. Behind it a black rider-less horse pranced along marking history with the touch of its hoofs onto the pavement. Mourners lined the streets. Many of us openly wept. Each in our own way shared the depth of the loss and recognized the significance of the silencing of this great American voice. As a nation we were all scared.

Life resumed, and I continued my not so illustrious career as a college student. My days and nights were filled with alcohol, Black Beauties, "No Doz," bridge games, dates with no sex, laughter, good times, close friends, boring classes, and dull, unenthusiastic professors.

All were large contributors to my emancipation into young adulthood and self-sufficiency. It was a breathtaking and thrilling experience, one that would end sooner than I had planned.

It seems that the faculty and administrative staff of my celebrated and distinguished Southern Baptist College finally had just about enough of me and all my accomplices. At the end of my junior year, after a fun-filled evening of drinking, dancing, and hiding in dark rooms with our boyfriends, we were shocked to find the Dean of Women waiting for us in the lobby of our dormitory. Individually we were escorted to our rooms and confined there for the remainder of the school year. We were each brought separately before Miss Neal. Questions regarding our whereabouts, our companions, and our liquor consumption were all directed at us in rapid fire. I have often wondered what must have been going through her mind as we each shared our varied, detailed and vastly different descriptions of the events of that night. Each of us was certainly attempting to save ourselves from her wrath and demoralizing attitude. Ultimately, my efforts failed. After completing my final exam, I was informed that my presence was no longer needed or wanted at Shorter College. It was a very long ride home that year.

I sat on this dismissal information for two weeks, endlessly pondering how I would divulge this unpleasant disruption to the completion of my college education. Mama and I would travel to West Virginia to visit my brother Jim and his wife. This seemed a much safer environment in which to reveal the sad news of the demise of my career and the end of a dream she had for me. I waited for the most opportune moment making sure Jim was available and able to act as a buffer. I confessed my sins, revealed the outcome of the tragic events and waited for my punishment. I did not fear repercussions against me. I feared and knew my punishment would solely and categorically be Mama's reaction. As feared and just as I expected, she wept into the night. My sleepless hours were spent consoling her and imagining any and all exit strategies out of my current educational dilemma.

Upon our return home, I quickly applied to Mercer University, a much larger Baptist school in Macon, Georgia. They were willing to accept a senior year transfer from another like-minded college, and I was set to begin classes in the fall. Mama was pleased.

Mercer was a full-fledged university with a well-established sorority system—one that excluded students from low income families, of which I was one. This culture of exclusivity provided a most unhealthy caste system. As a result, I was housed in the "outcast" dormitory along with the other low-income, unpopular, and excluded students. It was a most miserable period in my life.

There was, however, one bright spot without which I might not have made it through the year. That sparkle was provided by the magical voice of Barbra Streisand. I was obsessed and consumed by her. I knew way more about her than was healthy to know. When I felt suicidal, I played any Barbra LP. She would transport me to another place and my self-defeating, negative thoughts would float away with the sound of her voice. I collected every Streisand album for years and years. When CDs came into being I purchased all the remakes of her earlier albums and collected all the new ones. I finally ended my obsession and collection in the late 1990s. Her impact on my life, however, was definitely the most profound during that difficult senior year at Mercer University. I owe her so much, and she has no idea.

With Barbra's help, along with a multitude of Budweiser beers, I graduated in December, only six months later than previously scheduled. Mama was delighted.

I had no clear plans for my future so I decided to move to Atlanta, Georgia, in hopes of finding some clarity. I shared an apartment with three other friends in a new and hip complex filled with other restless, newly-graduated young adults. I took menial temp jobs, rationed food, and scraped each month to pay the rent. It was a time of much frivolity, drinking, dancing, and clubbing. Along with my staples of Ray Charles and Barbra Streisand, I began a new love affair with Duke Ellington and his unforgettable, "Satin Doll."

The anonymity of such a large city also provided the opportunity for adult sexual exploration. My first actual and complete experience was with yet another bad boy. This time I believe his name was Ken, although I must admit I cannot be certain of that. I was drunk. He was drunk. It was a most unglamorous encounter on the floor of our small, two-bedroom apartment. I was happy to have it behind me. It simply opened the floodgates for years of casual, unprotected and meaningless sexual encounters.

Soon I became impatient with the unfulfilling, carefree lifestyle I was leading. After a night of sloe-gin fizzes, vodka tonics, and white wine spritzers, the following morning I lay in my bed staring out into the empty parking lot. From this place of extreme hangover state, I had an epiphany. I remembered back to that Saturday afternoon long ago when my sister Sophia took me to see, "Destry Rides Again" at the Majestic Theater in downtown Philadelphia. The tap of the conductor's baton on the music stand as he called his orchestra to attention lay deep in my memory. The rise of the full length red velvet curtain aroused my senses and transported me to magical, mystical happenings inside my own mind.

I packed my belongings, drove home to Albany and the following morning told Mama I was leaving for New York City to pursue my childhood dream of a career in show business.

To say that Mama was stunned would be a misnomer. The look on her face suggested that she no longer recognized me. She was devoid of any awareness of that little girl she once held and came to control. Oddly enough, she did not stop me or attempt to stand in my way. I believe she was forced to confront the dilemma many mothers face when their child announces they are about to fly into the unsafe and unknown world of adulthood. We all recognize that it is the natural order of life and is as it needs to be. Yet it must be enormously painful for the one who birthed them, kissed them, cuddled them, nursed their wounds and healed their broken hearts since they were first held in their trembling mother's arms. God or Spirit provides many opportunities for the mothers of this earth to grow and learn and share a deeper kind of love, one that is like no other. That day, my mama stepped into that love and let me fly.

One's karma is an awesome aspect in one's life. It just IS. It is present whether we believe in it or not. I share this because I found it most ironic and mystifying that as I was about to make my long, unknown journey into my new life, my granddaddy found himself in the intensive care unit of our local hospital, Phoebe Putney Memorial where I was born. Mama, of course, said, "We are going to see him because this may be the last time." In all the years that I heard her utter those words, it seemed this time there was some validity to them. I agreed to go with her for a visit.

We wound through the hollow hallways filled with food carts, unfinished green Jello, and sodium-filled mashed potatoes. Nursing stations were busy with medical reports, and doctors were scurrying from patient to patient. As we reached the doorway to his room, I hesitated a moment before entering. I wanted to check my feelings before meeting my predator so as not to reveal our dark secret to our unknowing family. When I felt confident, I stepped into his unsafe domain.

As I watched him lying in the hospital bed, I wondered how it had all happened. How had this frail old man dominated me for years and so profoundly controlled my every move while in his presence? As I looked into his eyes, I knew his life was fleeting and set to make its exit in a matter of days. Casual conversation ensued amongst the gathered well-wishers and idle musings filled the air. I oddly found myself experiencing a sense of safety with my family and my aggressor in the same room. This was a first, and something I had longed for since our initial encounter. I recalled the feeling as my mama released my tiny hand that hot, summer day many years before. I recognize

A Legacy of *Lies*

now that this simple gesture had changed my destiny and, as I have come to understand, his as well.

As Mama was wont to do, she announced, with undertones of displeasure and pride, my impending relocation to the dark and mystical world of theatrical makeup, taxicab lined streets, and trains that run under the earth. All those assembled reacted with either shock, fear, or envy. While the debate pursued, I was stunned to catch the eyes of my granddaddy following me around the room. As our glances caught each other in midair, he raised his right arm, and with those familiar yellow stained fingers he motioned me toward him. My heart jumped as I recalled what that gesture had meant to me in our previous life together. Surely, there was no harm intended this day with a room full of witnesses present all tending to his every need. My breath slowed. My knees shook beneath my crisp Wrangler jeans.

I walked to his side, this time with my feet firmly pressed into the solid linoleum hospital floor rather than dangling helplessly from a four-poster bed. I bowed toward the frail, worn body that once had complete control over me and waited for his response. His breath was anemic, his voice just beyond a whisper. I found myself leaning over him as he had so many times leaned over me and into my innocent and fearful world as my dominator. I pressed my ear against his lips so as to gather his final words to me.

"Please don't go to New York City. There are bad people there. They will do bad things to you," he said without hesitation and seemingly without a conscience.

My dark, black eyes stared into his. Unable to speak, I silently backed away, my mind spinning with disbelief. I stared into his lewd and wanton face. No words passed my lips. Yet, I am certain he interpreted and fully understood what my silence meant. There was no further reason to respond. He did not, nor did I. Mama and I left that day driving home quietly, each in our own worlds. She was losing her father. I was walking away from a nightmare.

Several days later, I flew to Philadelphia where my sister, Sophia, picked me up at the airport. I stayed with her a short time and then traveled alone by Amtrak train to Penn Station on 34th Street, midtown Manhattan.

Granddaddy died. "Father, forgive them for they know not what they do?"

I felt nothing.

My favorite causes.

You can see I had already burned my bra.

Jeanne Hall

Looking for an acting job.

Nine

SODOM AND GOMORRAH

Another day passed with ease as I went about the chores of unpacking and putting my life in order after a visit with my family. As I went about these tasks, my conversation with Jim was not far from my mind. His was a simple question and the answer appeared so obvious to me. One only had to look into my life to see evidence that something damaging had happened that I carried with me. This evidence was reflected most vividly in the next stage of my journey. With my abuser now out of my life, surely I was finally free. Surely the yoke of his dominance was lifted as I escaped into the labyrinth of my new life style far from my antiquated Southern roots. Surely I was safe now.

It was New York City. Just like I pictured it, skyscrapers and everything. It was beyond thrilling to step off that train into the pulsating, vibrant energy of that grand Metropolis. I was stunned by the beauty of the tall buildings, the rush and push of the crowded streets, the

Sodom and Gomorrah

honking of the taxicabs, the smell of urine on the steps of the subways, the shouts of the street venders selling their wares, the flashing of bright lights on the Great White Way, long black limousines pulling up to stage doors, the homeless with their out-stretched hands blackened with the smut of the city. I had only dreamed of such magic, such adrenaline rushes. Here I was living that dream, walking in my fantasy, breathing in that vision. I ran down the streets absorbing all that my virgin eyes could hold and my awakened ears could contain. I was free to live as I chose. Free to know all that I could know, see all that I could see, speak all the words I needed to speak without fear or concern of impending harm. Surely I was now free to fly.

I would spend my first months sharing a studio apartment on East 24th Street with my cousin, Diane, the first born daughter of my Aunt Dottie, Mama's baby sister. Prior to my arrival in the big city, I had read a cover article in Time Magazine in which a "new" recreational drug called marijuana was introduced to the world. I was fascinated and vowed to give it a try as soon as I ran across it.

One night our downstairs neighbors invited Diane and me over to hear the latest Beatles' record, *Sgt. Pepper's Lonely Hearts Club Band*. Shortly after arriving, one of the young men, George, asked if we had heard of the new street drug marijuana. Remembering the article, I eagerly spoke up and without hesitation volunteered to give it a try. As was customary of the times, we threw pillows on the floor and prepared for an evening of new beginnings. George brought out a plastic bag from his chest of drawers containing the green and musty smelling elixir. Along with the marijuana he pulled out a packet of Zig-Zag rolling papers. I was fascinated by their distinguished logo of a mysterious, turbaned man holding a rolled cigarette and casually looking out at the consumer. As George began his demonstration of the proper etiquette and style of rolling a perfect marijuana joint, I remembered those years so long ago watching my granddaddy roll his Prince Albert cigarettes in the hot Georgia sun. I knew exactly what to do.

There is a bit of a learning curve if you have never experienced a toke from a marijuana joint. The first pull of the hot smoke into my lungs brought about a convulsive coughing episode that subsided only after a pat on the back from Diane and a sip of the hot brewing tea I found in front of me. Soon I understood the ease needed to lightly pull the smoke in with a slight sucking sound, holding the breath deeply and then releasing it full out with a satisfied, aahh. In keeping with the communal nature of smoking dope, the joint is passed 'round the circle from one person to the next allowing for some recovery time in between tokes. After a few rounds, I announced that I felt nothing and at the same time asked if there was anything to eat. It appeared that I was not the only one with a veracious appetite. George quickly offered his freshly baked chewy chocolate brownies. In true hippie form, these too were passed 'round the circle.

After everyone had settled into the glowing effects of the newly discovered cannabis, George placed the large *Sgt. Pepper's Lonely Hearts Club Band* LP onto the turntable and set the needle down onto the vinyl. The first strains of that psychedelic guitar jolted my ears. I sat straight up from my prone position on the floor eager for the first lyric.

"It was twenty years ago today,
Sgt. Pepper taught the band to play.
They've been going in and out of style.
But they're guaranteed to make you smile."

I was mesmerized as the crowd noises led us into "With A Little Help From My Friends" and "Lucy In The Sky With Diamonds." As I held the LP jacket in my hand, the marijuana high only intensified the psychedelic look of the confusing and crowded cover. Who were all those people and what were they all doing together? Why on earth was Shirley Temple standing in between Diana Dors and Marlene Dietrich? What were those stunning, majestic, multi-colored satin outfits, and why were the Beatles wearing them? My brain spun 'round and 'round and 'round, finding no answers—only more questions and not really caring either way. My first marijuana high, chewy chocolate brownies, the Beatles, and a night of freedom in New York City. What more could a small town Georgia girl want from her journey to independence?

Although I was far away from her, Mama was still a large part of this journey. As I traveled through all my new adventures I found myself thinking of her and longing to share my experiences. I called often to chronicle the new play I had seen, the acting or speech classes I had started, the new friend I had met. She welcomed each word from me with enthusiasm and wonder, and yet I knew she had never heard of any play I mentioned or knew the name of the casting director I had met the day before. I so wanted to be free of my childhood and yet deeply felt compelled to share it with the one person who was the anchor to that previous life. She seemed to enjoy hearing of my undertakings in the city, and I believe a part of her was living through me. My guess is that she would love to have had a few more adventures in her own life. At the same time, I also accept that my adventurous nature astounded her and left her wondering how I could possibly have been her child.

It was an altogether exciting time in my life. Having only seen westerns, horror flicks, and slapstick comedies at our local, small-town theater, or the drive-in theater on Slappey Drive, I sought out a more sophisticated array of movie viewing. I was introduced to the old Thalia Theater on the upper west side of Manhattan. I often took the Seventh Avenue train up for an all day stay in the darkened, art décor, broken-seated movie house. I saw my first Ingmar Bergman film. I met the stunning Greta Garbo and the sexy Marlene Dietrich. I was rattled to my core watching a young Marlon Brando pulling his hair out and screaming, "Stellllla." My world expanded, and I felt alive like never before.

New York City uncovered so much more than a thirst for art, theater, literary works of greatness, or a hunger for other cultures of the world. There was more than the multiple and varied ethnic groups who lived as my neighbors, shared the subways with me, and bumped into me while crossing 5th Avenue, as we all traversed the city together. Although these filled my soul, they were a mere sampling of what I was unblocking and allowing to unfold. Amongst all the glamour and majesty there were also dangers lurking in those same streets. Dangers that I found myself not only opening up to but actually seeking out.

    I had learned the art, the joy, the addiction of the adrenaline rush that comes from engaging in dangerous and illicit acts. My mentor, guru, sensei, teacher, the master, my granddaddy. I know this only in hindsight. While I was exploring my newfound, sometimes dangerous sexual freedom, I made no connections to the source of my addictions nor was I interested in discovering any. I simply gave myself over to and became an intensity addict.

    I took a job as a tour guide for the NBC studios in Rockefeller Center. My co-workers, all aspiring actors, producers, singers, writers or dancers, were seeking my same dream of fame and fortune in the Big City. I began acting classes on my days off and speech classes at night. My attention attracting, lilting Southern accent stopped people in their tracks when I spoke. This became a source of much shame and disgrace for me. I devoted my spare time to practicing all my vowels and consonants to reflect standard English pronunciation rather than revealing the stigma of my Southern roots. I moved to a small five-story walk-up studio apartment on the upper eastside on the corner of York Avenue. These small gestures provided a sense of stability and continuity in my life. My circle of friends expanded, and I continued to explore the city.

    Within this seeming tranquil yet exciting world, my heart held a secret I had shared with no one. Since those high school days with my friend H, I had wondered what it would be like to experience a woman in the fullest sense of the word. I was not close enough with my fellow tour guides to ask where I might find such activities. I was unwilling to expose this side of my life. I determined that the most likely source for this information would be the Village Voice. My instincts were correct. There in the back of the sprawling newspaper was a listing of all the Gay and Lesbian bars in the city. A number of them were located in the West Village so I knew my next adventure would take me there. I chose a Saturday night to begin my pilgrimage. As I sat in my tiny apartment, I realized I was filled with fear and would be unable to make this trip alone without some false, self-induced courage. To allay these fears, I quickly downed two shots of Tanqueray Gin, and armed with a new bravura, I jumped onto the Lexington Avenue train.

As I traversed the narrow streets of the village my fears mounted, yet my desire for this exploit grew more stringent with each step. Quickly I arrived at my first destination. Although I found the steps leading down to the basement a bit unusual, I hesitated only slightly before entering through the dimly lit door. Once inside, I noticed there were women standing at the bar, others gathered by the jukebox and still more rocked back and forth holding each other tightly on the dance floor. I was stunned to see that so many of the women looked just like men. This was not exactly what I had in mind. I found myself asking the question, where are the "real women?" I will attribute these judgmental recollections to my naivete and inexperience. I console myself by remembering that only months before I lived in the sequestered world of a deeply Southern culture. Women who looked like men, however, in no way daunted my excitement or curtailed my enthusiasm.

I walked to the bar and ordered a Budweiser in a bottle, a drink I deemed appropriate for the room. Soon the slightly illuminated, dingy underground bar filled to capacity. The noise level reached a fever pitched decibel level and the dance floor gyrated with a uniquely feminine motion. I joined that sea of femininity and lost my self in the group dance. I felt safe, exhilarated and finally, home. I danced 'til closing, drank too much, and left alone never giving out my number. No one was allowed that close.

Even while engaging in these escapades, I often felt the presence of Mama's watchful eye. She seemed to continue living inside me, traveling with me, participating in my adventurous follies, while sitting on my shoulder offering her judgmental opinion with a look of disgust. These "sightings" offered merely more than an annoyance. They in no way deterred my actions or altered my behavior. Their primary purpose was to provide a sense of guilt and shame that had a disturbing way of haunting me.

Aside from my selfish sexual concerns, I developed an interest in politics. The senator from New York State, Robert F. Kennedy was running for the presidency of the United States. I was deeply attracted to his courage, his compassion for the less fortunate, and his desire to make the world a better place. I joined his campaign.

During those busy days in 1968, tragedy again visited our nation. On April 4th of that year, Dr. Martin Luther King was struck down while standing on the balcony of the Lorraine Motel in Memphis, Tennessee. He was there to support the striking sanitation workers. Just the night before, he had given his famous "Mountaintop" sermon at a local Memphis church.

"I've seen the Promised Land.
I may not get there with you.
But I want you to know tonight,
that we, as a people,
will get to the Promised Land."

He indeed had not made it with us. I so longed for that conversation I could have had on that plane ride we shared so many years before. On April 9th, Mrs. King, with great dignity and grace, led the funeral procession through the streets of downtown Atlanta. It took my breath away. I carried my sadness with me through those days.

I continued my work for Senator Kennedy. His campaign was

gaining momentum. On June 5, 1968, he captured one of the biggest prizes in politics by winning the Democratic primary in the great state of California. While giving his victory speech in the ballroom of the Ambassador Hotel in Los Angeles, Robert Francis Kennedy was gunned down by Sirhan Sirhan. Once again, America watched as a great leader was assassinated, this time on live television. He died the following day at 1:44 AM.

On Saturday, June 8th, Kennedy's body traveled by funeral train from New York City to Washington, DC. The coffin was placed on a bier close to the floor of the car. It could not be seen by those who had waited for hours for the train to pass by. The pallbearers wisely lifted it off the floor and placed it up on chairs so that all who stood in the hot summer sun would be able to see him as he passed. Thousands lined the tracks as he made this final journey. I did not leave my house for days. I was devastated. That ended my life in politics.

Eventually, I did leave my house and life continued. My previous, rather uneventful evening into the Lesbian world of the west village was a faint memory as my desires began expeditiously to escalate. Soon I did give out my number to more than one unknown, attractive woman. With great ease and haste, I was fully on the road to "being out." My drinking increased and ultimately expanded into more marijuana and my first excursion into cocaine. I continued my relationships with men although alcohol was required in order to do so. I must also say that more often than not, I would leave a man in the doorway at evening's end, catch a cab to the village, find an interesting woman, and wind up in her bed before dawn. I created a vicious cycle of dangerous liaisons. Nothing filled me up.

I recall spending an afternoon at the Metropolitan Museum of Art strolling amongst the impressionists and soaking up the beauty of their captivating works of art. While sitting on a bench admiring a Van Gogh, a handsome young man took his place beside me. We exchanged a brief conversation on the merits of Vincent versus Gauguin and shortly we were on a subway heading toward his apartment on the lower eastside. After several hours of drinking wine, smoking dope and engaging in unprotected sex, I walked into the bathroom. There I found melting candles and multiple heads of porcelain dolls placed strategically on the bathtub and toilet. Although I was completely stoned, somewhere in my being I knew that this was not a safe place for me to be. In my dope and alcohol induced haze, I returned to his bedroom, gathered my clothing, never even knowing his name, and left his frightening, misogynist den of iniquity for the safety of the New York subway.

Even this encounter, although dazed by it, was not enough to curtail my dangerous rendezvous. It was not until I had lost complete control that I would begin to think about abbreviating these adrenaline-producing carnal encounters.

One notable evening began as they often did—a trip to the village, a night of drinking and snorting, dancing, flirting and then more drinking and snorting. Hours passed. I recall awakening the following morning in a single bed still high from the previous night's indulgences. As I glanced around the room, nothing was familiar. Instinctively I knew this was not my bed. I rolled over to find a woman lying next to me. I had no recollection of her name, who she was or how I had gotten there. Horrified in my drunken stupor, I once again gathered my clothing, exited the building and walked away never knowing this one-time lover's name.

Once on the street, nothing there was familiar either. I had no awareness of where I was. With cotton mouth, ruffled hair and twice worn clothing, I wandered the streets looking for someone who would be able to tell me where I was. It turns out I had made my first trip to Brooklyn. Unfortunately, due to my alcohol blackout, I had no recollection of it at all. My difficulties continued as I attempted to crisscross the unknown Brooklyn subway system during the hectic morning rush hour while finding my way back home to Manhattan.

Once there, I filled my bathtub with hot water and jumped in. While still intoxicated from the night's hedonism, I fell asleep as my head slipped under the warm, tranquil water. I was awakened only by my own choking and gasps for air as I struggled to expel the water from my lungs. I realized how quickly and easily I could have lost my life from my own self-inflicted asphyxiation, while enjoying that morning bath. I sat quietly reflecting on my life. I knew I was in trouble.

Clearly my own world had changed and expanded with each day, each year I lived and worked in the city. The world outside of my daily needs and excesses also appeared to be changing with equal fervor and passion. Just as individual growth can sometimes create apprehension and solicitude, I came to see that a nation can also experience angst and discomfort while confronting its provocations.

The raging Vietnam War dominated our nightly television screens. For the first time in our history, we saw the horrors of the battlefield in real time. We witnessed soldiers in body bags boarded onto planes, women and children ran naked in the streets fleeing the guns of their enemy, and bombs detonated on beaches while we sat and enjoyed our evening meal of Caesar salad and roasted chicken. Words like "collateral damage," the euphemism for the inadvertent yet totally unavoidable accidental killing of civilians, crept into the American lexicon.

While this manmade unpleasantness lingered on, the movement to terminate it forthwith grew in number and in volume. I joined in and proudly wore my "Send John Wayne to Vietnam" button to anti-war rallies throughout the North East. Every time I donned this prized button, I recalled all his cowboy movies I had seen sitting in the back seat of Mama's 1951 blue Ford at the Slappey Drive-In Theater.

One of the most memorable protests was held at Fort Dix, New Jersey. We gathered outside the huge base singing protest songs, holding hands, touting free love, passing joints around the massive crowd, never knowing what was actually in it and generally enjoying an "I'm a Hippy for Peace" day. It was a most enjoyable time until the local police force had had enough of the peace loving, pot smoking, unemployed youngsters occupying their hillside. Bull horns began blasting orders to disperse or risk being arrested. I must say we were given ample time to follow their commands, however, no one chose to heed them. We simply refused to move. I am not certain how much of our non-movement had to do with our commitment to world peace or how much was due to the fact that we were simply stoned from the pot and the heat of the sun. At any rate, their patience had dissipated, and we found ourselves confronted with the smoke and hideous smell of tear gas raining down on our peace loving, stoned-out heads. For my part, the concerns I had expressed for bringing our troops home and ending the Vietnam War were no longer a factor on that fun-filled day. My only thought at that moment was, "Run like hell." That is exactly what I did. Along with the other highly committed, fleeing protesters, I found my way back to the local train station, jumped onto the next train, and headed to the "smoky-air-so-thick-you-could-see-it," crowded Manhattan. There would be many other rallies, yet none quite as eventful as my day at Fort Dix.

Many causes germinated in the ripe breeding grounds of New York City that captured my interest and took hold of my passions. Women began speaking out. Imagine. Female writers shook our antiquated views of the woman's role in society. Questions were asked. As a people was it possible for us to expand our thinking to see women in a broader light? Was it appropriate for a woman to leave her traditional role in the home and join the work force? Was it acceptable for her to wear more provocative, appealing and stylish fashions? And the most comprehensive and compelling question, was it scandalous to change the national mindset to see that perhaps a woman could enjoy and long for sexual pleasure and satisfaction? The answer to all these questions was a resounding, "Yes."

My seeking mind longed for expansion and exploration as I sought out others of like mind. I soon found solace in such writers as Betty Friedan who had shocked the world and outraged many with "The Feminine Mystique." Ultimately her own outrage and that of many other women led her to write on a paper napkin at a conference in

Washington DC, the acronym, NOW. Thus began the formation of the National Organization for Women.

Gloria Steinem stood up and spoke out. I stood up with her and became an original subscriber to Ms. Magazine. I never used the English honorifics Miss or Mrs. again for myself or any other woman. I relished in the adventures and misadventures of Isadora Wing in Erica Jong's book, "Fear of Flying." Women everywhere began to take their fears with them and get on the plane anyway. We got on our "planes" at home, at school, and at work. The world listened and began to change with us. We were empowered.

I continued reading enlightening books. I burned my bra in Central Park along with other liberated women and made small efforts in my own life to take back my power. While working as a part-time bartender in a local pub in the theater district, my boss innocently asked me to wear more tantalizing, titillating outfits so as to encourage the male customers to stay longer and consume more alcohol. Incensed, I took my little white apron tied neatly around my waist, placed it on the bar, walked toward the door, and in my most liberated and empowered voice I protested, "You sir, can kiss my ass." Although I would without question handle a similar situation differently today, at that time, in that space I can assure you that I was enabled, entitled, and fully licensed to walk out the door. I did just that.

The 1970s was certainly a time in which the radius of our national consciousness expanded and amplified. Concerns regarding the hazards and dangers of nuclear power crept into our consciousness. The "No Nukes" mantra once again led many of us to Washington to protest our distresses and voice our opinions. All these causes fed our passions and led to an invigorating period of revolution, evolution, and true change that I welcomed and cherished. As each of us achieved our own human revolution and then jumped into activities that questioned the status quo, we were able to move the nation forward. I was rejuvenated and revitalized by the movements of that time, and they have strengthened me as a more socially conscious human being, and I am grateful for the privilege of my participation.

Life's dichotomies continued to glare back at me as I scurried about the city in my usual pursuits. By day I was ferocious in my acting classes, working my job as a waitress during lunch hour and rehearsing for my next Tennessee Williams or Eugene O'Neill scene for class. By night, I pursued the darkness of my carnal and addictive needs. Each carried equal weight and importance—the yin and the yang of life. I learned how to hold each of them in the light without having one be more or less important than the other. It was a sizable juggling act of which I became a master.

As I continued my studies, each acting part presented me with the opportunity to explore my feelings and to more deeply understand my place in the world and how I fit within it. I discovered there were many missing pieces, places inside my heart that had gaping holes, and mountains of longing for peace and release from my dark sadness. I decided it was time for me to experience this new psycho-therapy phenomenon I had begun to read about. I found a clinic that offered these services. Payment was based on a sliding scale according to one's income. I was accepted into the program. Since my income was quite meager, each session would only cost five dollars.

I was assigned to Dr. Hudson, an older woman who was kind, most gentle, and listened not so much with her ears but with her heart. In the beginning our sessions were filled with casual conversation rather than revelations. As I began to trust Dr. Hudson more, I unveiled circumstances around my relationship with Mama. We spoke of the love/hate connection that many young women experience with their mothers. I allowed myself to expose the mutual, unhealthy dependence that Mama and I shared. And after much thought and concern, we finally explored the meaning and repercussions of sleeping in the same bed with one's Mother for one's entire childhood.

These ways of living and developing did carry consequences that were playing out in my current adult relationships. Speaking of these controversies was enormously difficult and challenging for me. I instinctively knew there was more to be revealed and yet the fear of those discoveries was all-consuming. Soon my sessions became agony. I began speaking about unrelated subjects. I was baiting Dr. Hudson to extract the real issues from me. She remained patient during these months.

I am not certain why this particular day was the one for major breakthroughs. It had no rhyme or reason, yet one day it just happened. I exhibited my usual behavior for most of the session, then halfway through, I revealed my darkest secret. One never spoken of before. Prior to this moment, one known only to me. I confessed to Dr. Hudson and euphemistically to the world that my mother's father had been molesting me since I was a small child. As the words poured from my lips, I remember feeling nauseated, and gagging, choking in an effort to hurl out of my body this untoward secret. There was a stillness in the room. Dr. Hudson did not move a muscle. She allowed me to fully experience this cathartic event as though doing so would make it more profound and beneficial. After some time, she reached across her desk and without speaking, placed her hand on top of mine. I cried and cried.

I stood stunned on the crowded subway ride home that afternoon. I experienced all of the steps up my five flights of stairs as though each was another hurdle I must surmount. Finally arriving in my apartment, I fell onto my bed. I cried myself to sleep. When I awoke several hours later, I reflected back on my session and found that I was filled with rage. Rage not at Granddaddy. Not at me. This violence of feelings was directed at my dear Dr. Hudson, the only one who had ever tried to save me.

From a dark, sinister place in my mind, she had raped me in the same way that he had. She had forced me to reveal my deepest secret against my will. I was tormented within the malevolent walls of my own mind. The following day, I demanded another session. She accommodated my fury-filled request and allowed me to misdirect my granddaddy anger onto her as though in doing so we would experience some sort of poetic justice. Nothing she said appeased me. It was several weeks before I was capable of acknowledging that my anger was indeed misplaced. Dr. Hudson recommended I seek other means of expressing it. This seemingly simple task has turned into a lifelong search that has often resulted in careful containment and at other times resulted in massive explosions at the culprit.

The speaking aloud of my experiences with Granddaddy was a major breakthrough and came quite unexpectedly. Dr. Hudson had carefully woven her magic, creating a safe space for me to reveal little secrets after little secrets, one session at a time. Essentially she was training my psyche to take baby steps. Unbeknownst to me, I was gaining confidence so that on the day of the big reveal, I stood up and walked.

Even with this, I had not yet consciously made a correlation between the rapes and my devastating fear of being alone with a male without the aid of alcohol or narcotics. I was not yet aware of the connection between the loss of my daddy and my inability to allow anyone into my life on a meaningful and intimate level. The rather bazaar, co-dependent, caretaker, almost "lover" relationship with Mama had no relevancy for me. I did not yet understand the effects this might be having on my relationships with women currently in my life.

While sitting in Dr. Hudson's office, the only cognition I had was that I was about to completely implode or explode into unrecognizable pieces of nothingness. The pressure of holding these experiences inside for so many years had reached a critical mass and nothing could have stopped the events of that day. That milestone was merely the beginning. It was the touchstone for a life long journey into making the connection between those events and who I had become.

The intensity of my personal work was taking a toll on me, and I longed for an escape. One night it came to me in a vision. I would hitchhike home to Georgia. What else would a "starving actress" do for entertainment in the hot summer months but travel alone with only an army-green backpack and a few dollars in her pocket on the dangerous highways of the beautiful East Coast? My brain sizzles now when I think about that vision. Well, not so much about the vision but the reality that I actually did it, alone. Never in my wildest dreams would I attempt such a feat at this point in our society. However, at the time, I was armed with new found confidence that life with Mama could be better now that I had made some progress in my therapy. I believed I was stronger and would be able to find my place in her world.

I meticulously prepared, took care of personal business and headed to Penn Station. I took a train into New Jersey, exited after two stops and headed for the open road. Being the liberated, hippy woman that I was, I wore no bra and no makeup. My backpack contained one pair of jeans, one pair of shorts, two tee shirts, three changes of underwear and socks, a brush and tooth paste, macro-biotic raisins, and a bag of almonds. I decorated the outside of my backpack with my most prized buttons, "Send John Wayne to Vietnam," of course, my rainbow colored peace symbols, and my favorite of all, "Beverly Sills Is A Great High."

The first afternoon was exhilarating and freeing as I grabbed short rides from local residents—each one moving me closer to the hilly countryside of Pennsylvania. As the sun began to set, I became apprehensive with the realization that I had not fully planned out my sleeping arrangements. That part of my vision now appeared to be quite vague or non-existent in reality. It is important to note that cell phones and credit cards were a thing of the future. They did not currently exist as a safety net in times of need. I envisioned myself going off the road into the woods and cuddling up with my army-green back pack and Beverly Sills for the night.

Within a few minutes an older woman drove by and picked me up. I sat in the back seat as she lectured me on the dangers of a young girl traveling alone on the back roads of anywhere. She determined that I would spend the night with a nice family she knew in her neighborhood. They made a sweet dinner for me and bedded me down on their couch. I lay awake most of the night wondering if at any moment one or both of these nice family members might take out a kitchen knife and slash my throat. When the sun peeked through the trees in their front yard, I breathed a sigh of relief. We shared a breakfast of scrambled eggs and Kellogg's Corn Flakes before heading out to the nearest highway. As they opened the car door, the mother handed me a ten dollar bill, wished me well, and offered her prayers.

The simple pleasure of knowing that a crisp ten-dollar bill was residing in my back pocket was enough to make for a most pleasant morning. I might also point out that McDonalds and Burger King did not occupy the street corners as they do in our world today. The most prominent occupiers of those coveted street corners were gas stations, or as they were called in those days, service stations. Their name telegraphed their function and purpose for being. They actually provided service. One could drive their car up to the gas pump, and while remaining in the car, a service attendant came to the car window and inquired how they might help. Often they asked, "May I fill it up for you, Ma'am?" This same service attendant checked your oil, cleaned your windshields front and back, and looked at the air pressure in your tires.

The rest rooms did not require a key on a chain. The doors easily locked once inside. The floors were clean, the toilets pristine, the sinks had both hot and cold running water, and the brown paper towel dispenser was full to capacity while the trash can below was empty, as was befitting such establishments of the day. These sanitary lavatories were welcome respites for face washing and teeth brushing throughout my journey that summer.

Without the advantage, or disadvantage, of our current plethora of many and varied fast food restaurants, there was yet another phenomenon unique to the time. Every small town I visited had at least one Mom and Pop burger joint. One could order a hamburger and actually watch the "Pop" mold the red meat into a patty and toss it onto the grill. The "Mom" peeled and chopped authentic Idaho potatoes into large size pieces and dropped them into a cast iron skillet for frying. While you waited, yes actually waited, for the food to be cooked, you were offered a Coca-Cola. Long before the Pepsi and Coca-Cola advertising wars were waged, we called all sodas Coca-Colas. The effervescent, bubbly delight was served with ice cubes from a refrigerator tray delivered in a frosty, chilled glass. Heinz ketchup and mustard bottles were placed at each stool along with a bowl filled to the top with sweet, sugar cane granules. The four-foot-high stools were often steel on the base with cottony cushions covered in thick red plastic fake-leather. They were designed for efficient and carefree spinning while waiting for that homemade burger and fries.

Upon completion of your meal, you were presented with a check. It was generally written on a green tablet with a piece of carbon paper in between so that "Mom" and "Pop" could have a copy of the transaction for their records. A dollar-fifty plus tip covered my lunches most days on that adventurous solstice.

As the sun set each evening, I must admit that fear often entered into the quiet of my journey and jarred it to its core. Darkness on the road was not a welcome sight. Somehow though, I found a safe place to rest most nights. Camp grounds and trailer parks were abundant and people were kind and generous. I did, however, spend a few nights sitting straight up under a tree with my eyes wide open for the duration of the multiple night sounds and late night/early morning passing cars.

The dangers of hitching never really occurred to me until I encountered a cute but toothless truck driver somewhere in the hills of Virginia. Decked out with my army backpack and sleeveless summer tee, I set out for yet another day of adventure and exploration. While standing on the side of the road with the hoards of passing cars leaving my hair rustled and my breath short, a large semi-truck pulled over and the passenger side door swung open. I climbed up the high steps and entered the cabin. There I saw for the first time, the cute but toothless driver. All seemed casual and safe as he asked questions about my trip and my direction. I did notice, however, that his eyes often glanced down to the menagerie of buttons I was sporting on my summer tee. John Wayne and my rainbow peace symbol were most prominent. Suddenly he reached for my right nipple while remarking that he would like to grab my "little button and squeeze it."

In my mind, I heard the sounds from the shower scene in the film "Psycho," "Eeeekkk, eeekkk, eeekkk." I could see that knife-clutching hand slashing back and forth as Janet Leigh's blood swirled down the bathtub drain. Danger was imminent. Even with this image, I was thinking clearly enough to strategize an exit plan. The Gods were with me as we neared an exchange of roadways and my toothless driver needed to traverse from one to another. This prompted him to slow his speed significantly. As we made that wide turn, I grabbed my backpack with my left hand and the door handle with my right. The large door swung open with the force of the wind. I stepped onto the running board and leapt from the cabin of the moving vehicle landing on my side and shoulder in the firm Virginia dirt. As he grabbed for the swinging door I heard a loud and hostile, "Good riddance you stupid bitch." That was the last time I ventured into the cabin of any semi-truck, regardless of whether the driver was graced with teeth or not.

Although it was a fun summer, the hazards of the road became too much and finally near Atlanta, Georgia, I decided to find the nearest bus station and take the Trailways back to Albany. I safely arrived after a month of traveling. I was shower-less for days, makeup-less for weeks, and without a haircut for months. To say I looked like a hippie would have been an august distortion of my appearance.

The other travelers in the small-town, Anywhere, USA, bus terminal were ill-prepared for the Yankee flower child intersecting with their lives while waiting for their luggage on the side of the bus. I had become accustomed to the stares. Their fixated eyes served only to provoke and entice me to act more boldly and stare back with more fervor and disdain. Hippies rebelled against authority and anyone or anything that attempted to put us in a box or confine us. We loved being stared at, so I enjoyed my brief encounters with my fellow travelers. My pleasure was short-lived though as I made my way to the corner of Oglethorpe and Pine, where several drivers waited in their yellow cabs for a fare to anywhere. I knew that I had six-dollars and change in my back pocket. I inquired of the first driver as to whether the legal tender I possessed would cover the ride to 8th Avenue and the house where Mama lived. He assured me it would. I entered the back seat and headed for home.

Upon arriving in my childhood neighborhood, I asked the driver to let me off a block away so I could compose myself before knocking on the door. I had not let anyone know that I would be breezing in for an end of summer visit. I stood watching the front door from my neighbor's yard with short breath and a pounding heart. Soon I moved over to our yard and hid behind Mama's camellia bush. It was the same one she had jumped out from as she chased my bad boy Butch down the street. From there, I composed myself and walked to the front porch. My chapped hands and broken fingernails made a tight fist, and I gently knocked on the door.

I heard her rustle about inside. Her footsteps grew stronger and stronger as she drew nearer to a shocking surprise that she was ill-prepared to encounter. As she opened the door and saw me standing there, her face turned ashen from the impact. Her amazement must have been two-fold. One had to be the complete surprise that I was standing there unannounced on a hot summer day in August. The second surely was the trauma of recognizing the complete transformation of her "beautiful daughter" into the hippie, flower-child that she saw before her. Even with all that baggage, she opened the door and welcomed me in. Although it was not conscious, I do believe that a part of me delighted in her trauma and confusion. She no longer had control over me, and this was my way of rubbing it in her face—again, not consciously.

Over the next ten days, we tolerated each other. In her usual fashion, she dropped subtle hints about her displeasure with my appearance. In my usual new found fashion, I ignored her. I visited family and friends and attempted to make the most of my time at home. Then one night, everything changed forever.

After an evening with friends enjoying a few beers and some fine Southern pepperoni pizza, I returned to the house around eleven p.m. I noticed as I drove into the driveway that the lights to her bedroom were still on. I feared what this might mean as I quickly flashed on ways to hide the beer breath that I was sporting at the moment. I was relatively certain that I would be unable to quietly and easily slip into my bedroom unnoticed. My assumption was accurate. I opened the front door, turned the key to secure us for the night, and immediately heard her call my name. I had been had.

I walked to her bedroom door and queried as to how her evening had passed. She in turn asked about mine and inquired as to the well-being of my friends. We chatted for a few minutes and just as I thought I might escape to the solace of my room, she crashed through our fake façade and inquired about my appearance. Finally she had gathered the courage to just go for it and express her feelings about who I had become and why she found such displeasure with it.

In a most nonchalant way I engaged with her briefly, faking my true feelings and spouting inane explanations about the sign of the times. I was young and exploring. I used all manner of pseudo-concocted reasonings for my "outrageous" countenance. My words in no way diminished her fears. She appeared to have lost all logic.

Soon the conversation escalated to irrational accusations and character assassination. Inside, I shut down and allowed her to continue her impeachment of my intelligence and judgment. The tirade, however, soon swelled in my ears as though a symphony of timpani drums were being struck in unison.

"I never thought a daughter of mine would turn out looking like you," I heard her say through this symphonic haze.

Sodom and Gomorrah

With this, I stepped into another world. It was a world of slow-motion intertwined with rapid fire. My brain actually exploded into fragments of craziness. Without thought or scrutiny I yelled so loud my lungs felt on the verge of collapse.

"You are going to stand here and criticize the way your daughter looks—your precious daughter that you cannot even call by her name? You are going to criticize my very being, my very existence? I will tell you why. I will tell you why I am the way I am. Because all of my life, right in front of your face, *your* own father has been fucking my brains out."

My rage was overwhelming and engulfing. I deeply understood at that moment how convicted murderers claim they had no memory of the crime. I too have no memory of that space of time. My rage blocked my consciousness and left me in a vacuum of deep despondency. I actually could have murdered her and had no recollection of the event.

The room began to swirl and swing as though I were flying on a trapeze high above the big top. The only sound I heard was Mama's sobs piercing the free fall I was in.

"He tried it with me too," her frail and tenuous voice uttered through her wails.

With this she doubled over in pain and screamed. I could see that she was desperate, yet I showed no compassion.

"I remember that time when he was walking down the path with you and I came out to get you," she said as she gasped for breath and reached out her arms to me.

"Don't tell me this. Don't tell me this," I screamed at her still in a haze.

She was now completely out of control as well.

"I grabbed your hand and let you go. Is that when it started? Is that when it started?" she screamed back at me.

By her own account, she "gave me up to him." The pain was so excruciating that I completely lost control of my thoughts, my emotions, and my actions. I did "return" to the room at some point and watched her continue to wallow in her own pain.

"Don't you dare cry. Don't you dare fucking cry. This is *my* time," I shouted when I could take it no more and lost control again.

I left her room and returned to my own. I lay down on my bed and stared at the ceiling. I took no comfort in the knowledge that she too had been a victim. The room began to spin as it had so often in the past from over-indulgence in Budweiser or sloe-gin fizzes. Soon I threw up my pepperoni pizza along with a life time of pent up pain and anger. I stayed awake for most of the night.

With the sun's rise the following morning, I packed my belongings in my green army backpack still sporting my favorite Beverly Sills button and announced to my despondent mama that I would be leaving.

"Please do not write me. Do not call me. I am done," l shouted as I lost control again.

The long and sometimes tortuous bus ride back to the Port Authority in New York City afforded me the opportunity to review the events of my final night at home with Mama. I was filled with rage and deep disappointment. I was also consumed by the shock of learning that I was not the only recipient of Granddaddy's sexual urges. Were the occurrences between Mama and him frequent and to what magnitude? What was the time period in which the molestation took place? All were legitimate questions, however, my personal pain was too mountainous to have offered up an answer. At that point in time, quite frankly, I did not care. I was exhilarated to have liberated myself from her environment and felt a pronounced sense of freedom. As my long journey neared its end, I gazed out the Trailways bus window just before we ducked into the Holland Tunnel. The skyline of lower Manhattan and Lady Liberty raising her torch high above the choppy waters of the Hudson warmed my broken heart. I was home.

Upon my return to the city, I began yet another adventure. I walked into Stella Adler's Acting Studio to begin classes. Nothing would be quite the same again. I had heard about her and knew that

Sodom and Gomorrah

Warren Beatty and Marlon Brando had both previously studied with her. I was, however, ill prepared for the magnitude and impact of her presence. As we sat in class that first day anxiously awaiting her arrival, we nervously chatted with our fellow actors. Suddenly a hush fell over the room, the door handle turned and the most glamorous woman I had ever seen waltzed through the door, tossing her golden hair, and prancing like a queen to her throne. There she threw up her right arm as though reaching for the stars, lifted that angular, sculpted chin and in her most thrilling, powerful voice remarked, "Dawlings, Welcome to the Theatre." I was speechless. Her aura filled the tiny studio and seemingly spilled out onto the streets of Manhattan. Thus began our long, complicated, and fascinating relationship.

I grew up with her and the friends I met in those classes. We bonded in our love for her, our love of the theatre, and our respect for each other. I have come to see that we all loved her, hated her, couldn't get close enough, couldn't get far enough away, couldn't imagine life without her, and couldn't please her enough to satisfy our longing hearts. She was the gold standard in our lives and certainly in our acting careers. Upon reflection, she was the mother I always wanted and came to realize I had already had. My relationship with Stella was the mirror image of my relationship with my mama. She became my surrogate mother. All the things I wanted and needed from Mama I attempted to squeeze from Stella. My best guess is that most of us in her classes were squeezing her in the same way. I learned things from her that I still use in my daily life after all these years. She left a lasting impact on all of us and brought a new found stability to my life.

Time quickly passed and shortly, one year had passed since my last visit and communication with Mama. At that time, I saw no reason to change it.

However, during that same period I had a spiritual experience that would also profoundly alter my life forever. A friend invited me to a Buddhist meeting where I was introduced to Nam Myoho Renge Kyo. As we walked up the two flights of stairs to the apartment where the members were gathered, I could hear a hum and rhythmical sound of unified voices floating through the stairway. When we entered the small living room, I was shocked to see that there must have been seventy-five people kneeling on the floor. The energy was dynamic, yet light and filled with strength and joy. After the group finished chanting, not a word of which I understood, they sang songs and the introductory explanations began. Members shared their stories and experiences of how their lives had changed since beginning this Buddhist practice. I recall feeling completely at peace. As I watched quietly from my position on the floor, my heart knew I had found what I had been looking for. I joined that night with no hard sell or persuasion needed.

Within a few weeks, I was presented with a scroll called a Gohonzon. Focusing on this piece of paper, I was to chant morning and evening. It was to be carefully enshrined in my home along with an altar to respectfully honor my own life. I reflected back on the days I so dutifully sat on the hard, church pews and listened to Dr. Stevens urge me to confess of my sins. His oft quoted, "Thou Shalt Have No Other Gods Before Me" rang in my ears. His, however, was not the only voice that reverberated in my head. Mama's was loudest of them all. It was the two-octave-higher voice she generally used when she was most displeased with my behavior. Yet, here I was enshrining a foreign object with Sanskrit characters that looked very much like the scratches my daddy's chickens made in our backyard on Madison Avenue. Regardless of these current facts, I enshrined my Gohonzon immediately. I could hardly wait to get started with my new life.

I had heard other members share their stories of chanting for jobs, refrigerators, apartments, and boyfriends, as well as, many other sentient objects. Initially, I wanted no part of that. My chanting goals were simple. I wanted to become a happier person and relieve some of the pain I carried around with me as I negotiated through my life. My first night alone with my Gohonzon, I knelt on the floor and began to chant. I simply prayed to experience the loss of my daddy I had so neatly and securely tucked away that day in Mama's bedroom doorway. I was fervent and genuine in my plea.

Within a few minutes, I began to feel the emotions rumbling inside my body and quickly found myself sobbing without control. All the tears I wanted to cry that day when Clarence told me that my beloved daddy had gone to heaven finally found freedom and poured out of me that night. All the ways I allowed my mama to cry while I consoled and comforted her found a release and a vindication in my lament. The words never spoken, the sorrow never shared found a voice through my wails lying on that white, chilly, linoleum floor. I cried for three-hours, and I finally fell asleep using my kneeling cushion as a pillow.

As I continued my Buddhist practice over the next year, more was revealed, more was healed. My heart softened. I understood more, sought more and challenged more. I eliminated the conflict I had first experienced between Buddhism and my Christian faith. Both were valid and although vastly different in their dogmas and methodologies, they shared similar goals. I made peace between the two and gave up nothing.

Over this same period, I continued my weekly visits to Dr. Hudson. She had seen the changes and witnessed the benefits of our combined efforts at moving my life forward to a happier, healthier me. As we dug deeper into my psyche and I continued to survive it, one day she suggested that it might be time for me to open the communication with my mama. I had built my own unique, independent lifestyle. I paid my own bills, made my own money, stayed out late, got up early, had people over, went out dancing, sat home smoking, lived my life as I chose without restrictions. I made every effort to disassociate myself from my former life. I made certain to alter behaviors that were reminiscent of my Southern roots or would in any way reveal my past to a stranger. Once again, my "emotional rapist," Dr. Hudson, was asking me to allow myself to go deeper and wider to encompass more in my life. If I allowed myself to be vulnerable would I be able to have control within that vulnerability? I decided I could.

A Legacy of Lies

After more than a year of unreturned phone calls, rejected written communications, and returned gifts, I picked up the telephone and dialed my never-forgotten, long-unused home number. Although she attempted with all of her strength to hide it from me, when she recognized my voice, I "heard" her silent sobs. I am certain she had spent many nights on her knees asking God for this moment. Her prayers had been heard and now answered.

After a brief conversation, I invited Mama for a visit. She accepted with an open heart. We never mentioned our previous conversation or the events of the last night we had seen each other. I still cannot determine whether or not it was just too painful to recount those events and therefore I chose not to, or did my fear of disturbing the tranquility of the moment get the best of me? My final choice, in hindsight, was to simply move on. Regardless of the motive, we both did just that.

The date was set and the preparations were finalized for her arrival. I remember there was autumn in the air, leaves were beginning to fall from the trees in Central Park, the sun set a little earlier each day, the air was crisper in the mornings, and a cooler breeze flowed through the late afternoons. Again I was holding the yin and the yang of life. On the one hand I was excited to see Mama and share my exhilarating new life with her. On the other hand I was despondent and filled with fear that she would invade my private world. I envisioned her taking my life as though it was a kaleidoscope, freely shaking its mirrored tube while randomly changing the patterns, shapes, and colors of my new found independence.

Five days prior to her arrival I became violently ill. The usual symptoms of a flu persisted for two days, while I lost the contents of my stomach and all other microscopic particles seeking refuge in my other internal organs. The third day brought convulsive vomiting of green bile, seemingly from all orifices. I was unable to hold up my head or walk to the bathroom. My kitchen trash can served as the receptacle for the toxins leaving my body. I had never been that sick, nor have I ever been since. The day before Mama's arrival I stopped convulsing, was able to hold down some Campbell's chicken soup, and slept for most of the day. The following morning I showered, put on my happy—everything is wonderful face, and headed to La Guardia airport to greet my nemesis.

At the time of her trip, I was in my twenties and Mama was already in her late sixties. She was slower now though still quite healthy and spry for her age. There was a lovely, youthful spirit about Mama when she let herself go. It charmed all who witnessed it. She delighted my deepest sensibilities and my heart leapt with joy. Much to my surprise, we had a most glorious seven day escapade

Perhaps the grandeur and massive nature of the vibrant city awoke the carefree nymph in my mama. Or perhaps she simply let go of the Southern cultural pressure to act in a proper manner, to speak in a careful language and to touch only that which is deemed touchable. She had rarely traveled outside the myopic world of Albany, Georgia, yet she appeared ready for our Manhattan mystical tour. From the first steps of our journey, I realized that, as in most mother-daughter relationships, the tables had begun to turn. The child now was to become the teacher of the new ways of her world.

I introduced her to Greek Moussaka, Pad Thai from the Thai cuisine, Chinese Kung Pao chicken, and black beans with ripe fried plantains from the local La Cocina Cubana. She politely indulged me in all my offerings, yet in her heart I am certain she was longing for some fried chicken and corn bread. We visited the most famous and often-frequented tourist sites throughout the city. We traveled by subway to Battery Park and took a ride on the ferry out to the Statue of Liberty. The choppy waters of the Hudson River tossed us about while the wind blew gusts of the salty air and water into our faces. As was her custom, she took out the clear plastic rain cap she kept in her purse and quickly tied it around her chin. She was awestruck by the magnificence of "Lady Liberty," a symbol of freedom that until that day she had only experienced through a post card or in a magazine.

Another day we took the long elevator ride to the top of the Empire State Building. While looking out at the grandeur of the city, we pretended to be Alice Rae and trembled in fear wondering if King Kong would be paying us a visit that day. We stopped at the Russian Tea Room for an afternoon snack on our way home. That night I made her a salad in the tiny kitchen of my one-bedroom apartment, and we enjoyed a quiet time together.

In the culture of our small home town of Albany, Mama had not been exposed to any languages other than the uniquely Southern dialect she had grown up with and lived in all of her life. New York City by most accounts is the melting pot of the country. Multiple and varied systems of communication can be heard while shopping for a cup of coffee at the local deli on any street corner. To Mama, this was the most intriguing aspect of her trip. If we traveled on the subway, the people sitting next to her spoke in an unfamiliar tongue. Whether we dined at the local upper-Westside restaurant or the Rainbow Room on top of the NBC building at Rockefeller Plaza, no matter the location, new and original sounds fell on her ears. It became our charming little secret for the duration of our time together. When she overheard a new language, her face lit up like a candle in the night, her eyes lilted and she grinned from ear to ear making sure to catch my attention. I can still see that childlike look on her face and deeply cherish the memory of that shared time. On the days when I miss her the most, these are the things I remember and often long to experience again.

As we continued to explore the many sights and sounds New York City offers to its visitors and residents alike, we continued to also enjoy each others' company. We traveled by bus through Central Park to the Metropolitan Museum of Art spending an afternoon amongst the masters. We walked the short distance from my newly rented apartment on the Westside to Lincoln Center for the Performing Arts. There she gazed in awe at the heroic, mosaic murals painted by Marc Chagall that hang with grandeur in the lobby of the Metropolitan Opera.

Sodom and Gomorrah

Certainly most things that Mama witnessed and participated in while spending time with me were well out of her comfort zone. I would guess that if asked she might have even been repelled by some of them. Yet she traveled with me and shared in all I wanted to offer. It was a wonderful time even though I was often guarded and held close to the vest my true identity. Obviously, she was as well. I acknowledged the careful attention she paid to her words, the caution with which she approached our conversations. She was always careful not to allow an indiscretion or faux pas. We both protected our meticulously created and thoughtful tranquility. Nonetheless, it was a golden memory for both of us and one she spoke of frequently for many years.

She returned to her simpler roots, and my life in New York continued to excite and stimulate me on all levels. The spring following Mama's visit brought a unique opportunity for me. My mentor and theatre Goddess, Stella Adler, for the first time in her career, formed a repertory company using her students as the actors. I was fortunate enough to have been chosen to be a part of this select artistic assemblage. After tireless rehearsals and production preparations, we left the city for the New England states and our summer Thespian Adventure.

Our evenings were spent performing in the local theaters followed by cast parties hosted by the local intelligentsia and admirers of the arts. For me the crowded rooms filled with fawning and inquiring strangers were equal to torture chambers with dripping water facets and fingernails screeching over chalkboards—agony at its most dramatic. I would say they were torturous at least until I had consumed a few glasses of champagne, or a Tom Collins, or a minimum of two chilly gin-and-tonics. My fears were thus pacified, and the gregarious, vivacious other personality appeared and carried the night.

As is the life of young, yet undiscovered actors, after our wonderful summer of touring, we all returned to the city unemployed and looking once again for interesting ways to pay our rent. With my previous though limited experience, I was hired as a bartender. It took only a few days to recognize, once again, that this would not be a career worth pursuing.

I next found work as a cashier at the Metropolitan Museum of Art where I spent my lunch breaks with Rembrandt and shared afternoon tea with Van Gogh, Dali, and often times Monet. Then one morning, I discovered the Jules Bastien-Lepage's Joan of Arc glaring back at me from the mammoth gallery wall. Her larger than life presence and penetrating blue eyes captivated and inspired me. I used her as a champion to those who defy all odds and succeed with courage to slay the demon dragons. I still carry a post card of her to remind me to stay strong in life's storms.

In between auditions and small acting jobs, I further pursued my cashier career at the famous Cinerama Theater on Broadway. There were two benefits to this job. For "starving actors" money is an issue which means that food is also an issue. As long as I worked in the theater, I was guaranteed a dinner of freshly popped corn served with unlimited drinks from the soda fountain. Many nights, this was the only food I had.

The second benefit of working at the old Cinerama was found after the audiences left the house. The manager of the theater was a handsome young gay man who shared the managerial duties with his young, handsome gay lover. After the last patron left, I ran up the long aisles to lock all the doors and secure us safely from the outside world. His partner stepped into the projection room, pressed a single button and the towering Cinerama screen lifted up and disappeared into the ceiling. The manager pulled a freshly rolled marijuana joint from his briefcase. I opened the bottle of wine I had smuggled in, grabbed some paper cups from the concession stand, and the three of us shared the intoxicants. Within a short time, we were all three high as kites.

With that, we put the sound track to the original musical version of the Broadway smash "Mame" into the colossal audio system. The overture began. My two handsome, gay friends exited the realties of our mundane New York lives and stepped into a fantasy world of song and dance on that massive, beautifully curved stage. I was the gleeful, screaming audience. My dear intoxicated female impersonators sang every note and passionately danced every step of Auntie Mame's big adventure to my utter delight. Perhaps someday a gifted, innovative Broadway producer will recognize the brilliance of this and bring an all male version of Auntie Mame to the Great White Way. I relish in the knowledge that I could always say I saw the original version

I next took a job modeling full length sable and black chinchilla coats for a manufacturer in the garment district. I was not at that time enlightened to the horrors of harming these stunning creatures for the satisfaction of the vanity and ego of women around the world. I would certainly make a different choice today. At the time, however, I must admit it was quite a thrill to strut through the showroom, spin elegantly in front of the buyer and with a dramatic flair drop the coat to the floor, exposing the pelts of sable in their most glamorous and alluring way. Somewhere inside I began to think about those gorgeous animals and that my actions were promoting an industry I was not emotionally in alignment with. I decided it would be better for me to find another way to pay my rent.

Soon after the demise of my modeling career, while searching through the New York Times Sunday classified section, I spotted an offering that tweaked my imagination. The ad read something to this effect:

Looking for glamorous girls to Escort Gentlemen
for an evening out on the town.
Earn up to $100 per night.

For a starving young actress this was an opportunity too enticing to pass up. The following morning, dressed in my most glamorous attire, I walked into their offices on East 56th Street. Contrary to popular belief, the young business woman actually envisioned an escort service for men who visited New York from around the world. She hired me on the spot with a stern reminder that the only services I was to provide were those of escort. Any other extra curricular activities provided would result in my termination.

I had my first escort the following week. As promised, I met the gentleman at the Waldorf Astoria Hotel, had a lovely dinner, followed by a Broadway show and dancing 'til three in the morning at a disco club, after all it was the late '70s so disco it was. At the end of the evening, he hailed a cab for me, gave the driver a fifty and slipped a hundred dollar tip into my hand. I drove off into the night.

I developed regular customers who requested my company when they were in town. Yet these late night excursions began to put unwanted pressure on my psyche and ate away at my sense of well-being. I recall in particular a night with one of my regular "gentleman callers." We had an exciting evening, the usual fine dining, Broadway show and drinking and dancing 'til two. As promised and agreed upon earlier, he hailed an eagerly awaiting taxi, slipped me the obligatory hundred dollar tip, and off I drove down Fifth Avenue. Rather than heading home, I directed the driver to my favorite Lesbian bar on Christopher Street. In my alcohol-induced state, I found another willing, though intoxicated, partner for the night and woke up, once again, wondering what I was doing and why I was sleeping in the bed with a stranger.

One of my last transient jobs was as a waitress in a trendy, upper west side bar and grill near my home. I could ride my bike to work and generally pick up a hundred dollars in cash along with a free meal. A meal that was quite a step above my previous pop corn and soda at the Cinerama Theatre, although the entertainment was nowhere near the same caliber.

One night after closing up, I hopped on my bike and headed to 72nd Street. I was riding with the traffic, which put me very close to the parked cars along the street. Midway through the block, I heard someone calling out to me from the sidewalk. My thought was that perhaps I had dropped something from the back of my bike. I slowed and turned to see a tall figure waving at me. For reasons far beyond my understanding to this day, I felt compelled to reverse my course and head towards the stranger. As I met him he offered some excuse as to why he had called out to me. At the time it seemed important to me and whatever his concern, I offered to help. I willingly followed him into the doorway of a nearby building.

Once inside he offered me a drink. At that point I was a willing prey. Asking me if I wanted a drink was like asking a drowning woman if she wanted to be thrown a life preserver. I took the drink. We chatted about his life, his family, his wife. He in turn graciously asked questions about my life and career. It was actually quite pleasant.

After several drinks I noticed the time. I thanked him and prepared to make my exit for home. As I turned to grab the door handle, my stranger in the night, grabbed my arm and swung me around to face him.

"You are not goin' anywhere," he said with fire shooting from his eyes.

I attempted to pull away. He was a very large man and much stronger than me. My efforts were futile.

"You are not leavin' this building until you suck my dick," he said while holding my arm even more tightly.

Terror was now setting in. I began to panic but found enough strength to try once again to escape. As I reached for the door, he grabbed me from behind and threw me to the floor. In a single fluid motion his imposing hands were firmly wrapped around my pulsing neck. My attacker was now emboldened.

"You are going to pay for the deaths of Bobby Kennedy and Dr. Martin Luther King. Somebody has got to pay and you are it," he shouted from his position of power.

I understood and felt first-hand his black rage. How could he know that I too had cried for someone to pay for the deaths of these great men. I too wanted someone to lift the pain of these losses from my heart. At the same time, I knew that this information would in no way console my late-night abuser. I weighed my options. I could follow his instructions and satisfy him sexually, or I could risk losing my life to this unknown abductor by continuing to resist. The latter would most certainly lead to my becoming yet another statistic. The headline in the New York Times Section D would read,

Young girl from small town falls prey to the dangers of the big, dark city.

And then my granddaddy would have been right.

I made the decision to give myself up for his violent, carnal satisfaction and in turn save my own life. At that time I did not consider the possibility of any other outcome. Now I can see that often in these situations, the seduced may comply with all the wishes of her predator and in the end still lose her life. I am grateful that these thoughts escaped me that night.

As my ordeal continued, we moved from the floor to a chair and back to the floor again. In his case, once was certainly not enough. I followed with great care, all his instructions. The fear of finding those large hands wrapped around my neck made me appear to be a willing participant. Finally, he was done. I prepared to leave. As I reached for my purse, he once again grabbed my arm. Terror set in again. This time, however, he reached for my wallet and removed my identification revealing all my personal information. He had obtained a weapon that he believed would prevent me from reporting our evening to the NYPD.

"You tell anyone about this, and I will hunt you down like a dog," he quietly and dispassionately remarked.

He straightened his clothing and walked me out to the street.

In the strangest of behaviors, he now insisted that we share a meal together in a local restaurant as though all of this had just been a lovely evening enjoyed in the thriving metropolis of New York, New York.

Sodom and Gomorrah

Oddly enough, his choice of restaurants was the one in which I had introduced Mama to Cuban Cuisine on her recent visit. While he pretended that all was tranquil and normal, I appeased my fears by reflecting fondly on the evening Mama and I shared together not that long before. I recalled the look on her face as she tasted for the first time the spicy, jerk chicken. These recollections soothed me, and the time passed quickly.

After completing our meal, he paid the bill, and I prepared to make the short walk to the safety of my home. To my surprise, my provoker refused to allow me to take this walk alone. He insisted that he join me to offer protection from any harm that might come my way. It did not escape my awareness that my most aggressive of molesters, my granddaddy, had offered a similar cautioning from his hospital bed. My current molester insisted that I walk the streets while he drove my bicycle in circles around me all the while laughing and taunting me. As I saw it, his goal was to degrade, humiliate, humble, and bring me to my knees. He succeeded on all counts.

Finally we arrived at my apartment. My antagonist returned the bicycle to me, thanked me for the evening and reminded me that he still had my identification and knew exactly where I lived. I climbed the five flights of stairs, turned the key and stumbled into the safety of my tiny studio apartment. Out of desperation, I walked into the bathroom and turned on the shower. I stepped into the tub and allowed the warm, cleansing water to flow over my body. The sweat and semen left by my strange invader swirled and finally disappeared into the awaiting drain taking with it the only real evidence I had of my night of horror. When the sun rose, I slowly dressed and walked to the upper Westside police station.

Once there I shared my story. I had never heard of a rape kit and therefore did not know what it could mean to the case against my abductor. There was little hope of finding a piece of fiber or a strand of hair left behind. DNA was not yet a tool to be used in confirming one's involvement in the commission of a crime. All I had was my word and his name that he had willingly given to me in our early conversation. Although he now had access to all my personal information, in his arrogance he had ignored the importance of the details he had shared with me.

Within the hour my rapist had been picked up from his place of business and brought into the dingy upper Westside police station. From behind a one-way mirror I immediately identified him. Although he was questioned for hours, he stuck to his story of innocence. He was ultimately removed from the room and released to return to his peaceful, family life. I was left with the thought that he would find me again and would complete what he had started that night.

I was not privy to the conversations held behind closed doors between the police officers and my rapist. I was, however, assured that I would never see or hear from him again. I was escorted home by a nice young officer. Their words of assurance did little to assuage my fears. For months, I looked behind every door, froze with every sound and stopped for no one. Yet, he did not appear. I have no idea what they did or said to him at the station that day. I do know that they were true to their word. I never saw or heard from him again. Just another mystery of behind the scenes police work.

Once again when tragedy struck in my life, I shut down. I did not cry. I did not rage. I did not feel anything. I was numb. I put the dark episode into my back pocket with no particular focus and proceeded with my life. I was unenlightened as to the effects such events might have on one's life. Were they in any way contributing to my unconscious victim mentality? Or on an even deeper level had I drawn this event into my life because that pattern had already been established from my encounters with my grandfather? These are questions that came only with hindsight. At the time, I pretended all was well in my world while continuing to anesthetize my wounds with daily sedatives of drugs or alcohol. Most often it was both. I was a docile yet ticking time bomb.

I gathered my internal bruises and proceeded with my life. Buddhism became my safely net. I threw myself into study and came to see what it meant to respect and honor another person in a deeper, more profound and complex way. I learned that my happiness could be found only from within my Self. I painfully came to cherish the concept that I was the only one responsible for my actions. As my involvement deepened, my career became less and less important to me. I realized that in order to truly succeed I would have to want it more than anything else in my life. I began to see that I did not.

As my life expanded and I understood more acutely the Buddhist concepts, I longed to share these changes and understandings with Mama. At the same time, I knew that there was nothing about these traditions that would be pleasing to her. The Southern Baptist roots entrenched within her being would rebel against all the rituals of my daily practice. They would be deemed slanderous and sacrilegious. I hesitated and thought carefully before sharing my newfound theology with her. In my naivete, I had hoped that she would see the differences in my life, acknowledge them, and accept them as worthwhile and meaningful to me. Nothing could have been further from the truth.

In our opening conversation, I gently and with the greatest concern chose my words with care. Initially there was no response on the other end of the phone. I imagined her holding the headpiece away from her ear so as not to be contaminated by the words that spewed from the other end. In her most outraged tone and with righteous indignation, she refuted my every thought and theory. The level of her voice bordered on hysteria and was nearly out of control. She was stunned that I would forsake my religious roots and allow a false God to take over my life. There would be no meeting of the minds that day or any day thereafter. All the concepts and traditions of my newfound spirituality became a thorn in her side. I believe that in her mind I had literally and figuratively crucified her. All was blasphemous. All went against her God.

Finally, I was wise enough to realize that I was in a losing battle. I raised the white flag and with my dignity still in tact. I retreated to silence and a world of nondisclosure. Without anger or hostility I terminated the conversation. We would not speak of it again for years. I continued my quest for self-evolvement and personal enlightenment on my own and without fear. I came to see that my God was also her God, simply given another name.

Soon I began to long for more stability in my life, particularly in the financial arena. The days of struggling to pay the rent, pounding the pavement to catch a break, getting that envied audition or making a connection with a promising talent agent, all began to drain and weigh me down. Could I put aside my long-dreamed-of career as an actress and pursue a more stable occupation? Shortly my question was answered, and my destiny shifted in a heartbeat.

I took a "real job" as a producer in the radio and airline entertainment division of Billboard, the most prestigious record industry magazine. Soon I was promoted to Producer of the American Airlines' account and found myself flying around the country meeting the most prominent musical stars of the day. The beauty of the experience was that one day I might interview Leonard Bernstein in NYC. The next day I was heading to Nashville to chat with Barbara Mandrell, then on to Los Angeles to spend an afternoon with Quincy Jones. I traveled so frequently that often while running through an airport to catch another plane, I would wonder to myself, "Where am I?"

I do vividly, however, recall my interview with Stevie Wonder. We had a lovely conversation. We laughed and enjoyed each others company. We were nearing the end of our time together.

"Hey, let me take you for a ride in my new car," Stevie said as he jumped up.

Had time permitted, I would have taken that ride along Riverside Drive in Burbank, CA, with Mr. Stevie behind the wheel. That is an adventure I am sorry I missed.

On that same visit to Los Angeles, magic struck and changed my destiny. While in the Billboard office, the chief sound engineer of the LA Studio resigned to return to radio. I literally was just standing there.

Sodom and Gomorrah

"How would you like to move to Los Angeles?" the head of the department said as he turned to me.

"You pay me my asking salary, move all of my belongings, set me up with housing and I am in," I replied, armed with an unknown, heretofore never recognized courage.

"You're in," he said without hesitation.

I returned to New York, packed up my apartment, said my good byes, loaded up the Mayflower truck, and flew to my new home, Los Angeles, CA. When I made my decision that afternoon, I gave no thought to what it would mean for me to leave behind my beloved New York City. My teacher, my comforter, my addiction, my rush.

I dismissed the clamoring of the subway trains as they sped along the tracks leaving a blast of hot, steamy air brushing against my face and the piercing sound of metal on metal as the brakes were applied before shrieking to a halt at each station. I disregarded what Sunday mornings might be like without lying in bed with the New York Times calendar section, a pot of hot French Roast coffee, and a slice of an Entenmann's Cheese Danish. I was ignorant of what life would be like without walks through Central Park on hot summer evenings catching a soft ball game between cast members of Broadway shows or what it would mean to leave behind my strolls through the towering galleries at the Metropolitan Museum while my eyes feasted on the great masters' works of art. I discounted those evenings I wandered into the theater district, waited in line until curtain time and purchased a standing room only ticket for five dollars. I set aside the plethora of exotic and intriguing cuisines that were available to me within a short subway ride uptown, downtown, or cross town. I left behind the thrust and united forward motion of the crowd as the light turned green on any street corner. I abandoned the power of holding my arm high into the sky, hailing a cab and as the driver screeched to a halt in front of me, jumping in as others watched and with great authority exclaim, "Fifth and 51st, please."

My abrupt, somewhat careless choice was made without thought to any of these lusts I so deeply needed, craved, and longed for. My voracity for adventure took control of my body that day and altered my life dramatically and with finality.

Ten

THE GARDEN OF EDEN

Through the adventures of my life in New York, it became clear that Granddaddy's demons followed me through the streets. I recognized this in the depth of my being as I reflected on my life and searched for more evidence for my brother Jim. I wanted so to pursue an answer for him, yet my fear of what I might find was far too great. I needed more time to contemplate what I would do next. I retreated to the woods of beautiful Tennessee and walked for hours. My mind turned to the next adventure on my journey.

In my initial viewing, Los Angeles appeared to be a single-hued palette. As we drove through the city my first afternoon, I was struck by the awesome beauty of the environment and yet stagnancy persisted at the same time. We drove from the beaches of Santa Monica to Sunset Boulevard and wound our way through Bel Air and into Beverly Hills. Stunning red bougainvillea draped the pristine white stucco facades of the movie stars mansions that lined the streets. Palm trees rose above us, reached into the cloudless blue sky and swayed gently in the afternoon breeze. Ominous steel fences with tightly secured, locked gates said to passersby, you are not welcome. Long, black limousines rolled through the boulevards. Eyewitnesses were prohibited from viewing those hidden behind their portentous tinted windows.

The women strolling the sidewalks of Rodeo Drive were fit, blonde, beautiful, stylishly dressed, and oozing with panache. The delicately tanned men dashed about with turned up collars and sexy sun shades shielding the lust that lay in their eyes. Lamborghinis and Ferraris roared past us leaving me to wonder why. What purpose these magnificent machines served dashing through the hoards of other bumper-to-bumper automobiles remained a mystery. Perhaps it was that deep need to fit into the ostentatious and conspicuous culture that ran helter skelter through the streets of Los Angeles.

This sanguine, idealized, and misguided view of my new home left me empty and melancholy. A cultural demarcation was clearly laid on the hot pavement that mysterious afternoon. A class war waged in those immaculate, sterile streets. I would soon learn that all was not unsullied or sterilized. LA would indeed show its true colors. It would take some time, however, my eyes would indeed open to view with clarity a beautiful multi-colored palette of varied, diverse cultures and lifestyles. It was very different from my beloved Manhattan, yet, still intriguing and arcane to its core.

At first glance though, the glamour and dazzle of this new lifestyle became a touchstone for all that was addictive and compulsive within my being. These peculiarities functioned as a magnet to pull me more deeply into the dark abyss of Hollywood decadence. The sleek, stylish convertibles, the tight golden bodies, the rolls of cash held snuggly by silver money clips, the alluring and provocative nightlife, bringing with it the availability of freshly harvested, uncut, pure cocaine and the finest Dom Perignon, all served as intoxicants—intoxicants over which I seemingly had no control.

It reminded me of the parable in the Genesis chapter of the King

The Garden of Eden

James version of the Bible that Mama kept by her bedside table. As the story is told, Adam and Eve lived in a paradise filled with natural beauty and tranquility. Plump fresh fruit hung languidly from the lush trees. Honey was to have freely flowed from mountainsides while bluebirds flew overhead. In this unblemished world, Adam and Eve ran about uncorrupted and immaculate. All was well and good in their wonderland until the lewd and lascivious reptile appeared before Eve and attempted to debase her innocence.

Even as a child, I had wondered why the snake appeared before the female. It seemed to have been the genesis for the myth of female untrustworthiness that has followed us since the beginning of time. Nonetheless, he was indeed able to tempt our angelic Eve with the bite of an apple thus changing the course of history for all humankind.

Los Angeles was my wonderland, my Garden of Eden. Cocaine flowed freely from the mountains of Santa Monica and sea gulls flew over the Pacific Ocean. A lewd and lascivious reptile never actually appeared before me; however, many beautiful, tightly-toned women offering drugs and the finest of alcohols did. Unlike Eve, I did not have to ponder my decision nor reflect on the results that my actions might bring. I jumped in full force with no thought of the consequences and fed the needs of my addictions like a ravenous jungle lioness.

Even with all these temptations I passionately jumped head long into my new job. Its challenges stirred my imagination. It also lent itself to feeding my obsessions and satisfying my multiple needs. Power lunches with martinis followed by wine and sambuca were daily events. My life became the Garden of Eden, only in my story the lewd and lascivious reptile lived there with me. I generally invited him to sit down for afternoon tea.

After some months and more exploration, I began to daydream about what it would be like to share my new world with Mama. For much of her life she had been moonstruck by her vision of Hollywood. We shared that need to escape into its fantasies. She was delighted to answer my call and set about making her plans to visit.

She arrived in early October so as to avoid the heat of Los Angeles summer days.

Our time together was sweet and loving. I took her picture in front of Grauman's Chinese Theater while she placed her hands in the palm prints left by Clark Gable or Rhett Butler, as he was known to her. We drove up California Highway 1 to Hearst's Castle and spent a day touring its grandeur and sharing in the illusions. That day she wore a pastel blue polyester pantsuit and her familiar plastic rain bonnet to protect her coiffure from the salty ocean winds. We traveled to the desert, where she stood in the red and yellow poppy fields and giggled like a child. We spent an afternoon at the recording studio at Billboard's office on Sunset Boulevard. I put her in the sound booth and interviewed her as though she were the hottest new singing sensation. She laughed with abandonment. I introduced her to Surf & Turf at Moonshadows Restaurant on Pacific Coast Highway while the sea pounded against the rocks as the glowing red and golden sun set in the west. We chatted casually as I envisioned many mothers and daughters do while sharing time together.

I reflected on the normalcy of the evening and yet for us it took on an air of magnificence. Rarely had we conversed with such commonality and sensibility. She asked for no particulars about my life. I volunteered none. We traversed our time together in harmony, with minimum walls, lovingly, and with great care. She returned to the South as quickly and as easily as she had arrived retreating to her world and leaving me to mine.

During these years, even within the seeming chaos of drugs and alcohol there was stability in my work and strength within my Buddhist faith. One concept in particular had a piercing effect on my way of thinking and experiencing the world. Basically it states that we cannot separate ourselves from our environment. If we look into our lives and are unhappy about what we see, rather than complain or blame others, we have the power and the choice to take actions that will bring a more pleasing result. I made my best effort each day.

The Garden of Eden

Regardless of these gains, living inside my mind and body was an extraordinary experience. There was anarchy from within. On one hand I had enormous power, mammoth energy, astute, clear thought with a quick wit. Often I felt invincible. At the other end of the spectrum was the delusion, the madness, the tortured sleepless nights, the explosive rage directed at no one, yet pulsing inside my veins, the paranoia coupled with the psychedelic roller coaster ride of extreme, acute emotions, all splitting my mind into tiny pieces. I could find no peace. I lived it everyday. With my Buddhist practice I stayed on my course to find inner tranquility and reach agreement amongst the anarchists running recklessly and haphazardly in the walls and deep crevices of my gray matter. I often felt as though all my desperate efforts were keeping me afloat with small increments of forward motion. In some small way, however, it satisfied me. I relished in the comfort of knowing that I was no longer slipping backwards nor sinking to the bottom of the pool of life. I was at least maintaining.

Thus were the contrasts of my existence. I came to see that often we paint a picture of ourselves, one that we present to the world. We carefully choose the textures and our tinted shades giving each the value we determine it deserves. We do not offer our "me" gift to be examined, delved into and scrutinized. It is merely our contribution to the collective consciousness. It is one that we trust will fit in with the others and be a stronger link in the chain. To my outside world, no one was witness to the tormented, tragic figure that occupied and commanded a dual role in my being. This inward character stood side-by-side with the strong, courageous, and outspoken persona I proffered to those who dwelled within my domain. These dualities were known to me. They became commonplace—bringing with them a sense of calm and safety. I never once questioned how I arrived there. I did not seek for the origin of my rage. I did not look for the genesis of my need to be the victim wherever possible. I simply carried my dualities with me and lived my life in LA as I presumed all those negotiating the streets of Hollywood did.

One afternoon navigating these roads in my brain, I received a call from Mama. She had not felt well for some time. Following a series of tests, she had been diagnosed with lymphoma. She was referred to an oncologist who was to design a treatment plan of extensive chemotherapy and radiation. At the time, this information had only a minimal impact on my life. I was concerned of course, however, I had no experience with chemotherapy or radiation, its effects on the recipient, or the impact lymphoma had on a body. Somewhere inside though, I knew that Mama was already in her 70s and that this would not be an easy road for her.

My life in Los Angeles was full and rich in many ways. Mama's illness was a distraction yet also an opportunity to witness the benefits from the faith I had chosen to live by. I had spent so much of my life caring for, being concerned about, and pandering to Mama's every need. I came to see that a part of me wanted and expected my brother Jim to take over those reins. He now lived in our hometown and had flexibility in his work schedule so could be available for treatments and needs that Mama might have.

Through this cognition, I came to see that I still harbored resentment, anger, and hurt that I had carried over the years while sharing our journey together. A part of me felt that I had done my duty. Let someone else take over now. It is quite awesome to see how we as humans can hold unconscious resentments and ill feelings and not attribute them to any particular situation. I did not in my conscious mind connect all the years I slept in her bed to appease her loneliness, nor the numerous occasions she locked me out of the house because my actions did not please her, nor how frequently I gave up my own feelings in an effort to comfort her, nor the times I held back my own tears so that she could sob in my arms. None of these connected to why I was unavailable to make the long trip from Los Angeles to Albany, Georgia. I rationalized that I was simply too busy with so many, many important things, and it was just not wise for me to leave all my responsibilities behind. I deeply regret my actions.

The Garden of Eden

Unaware of my neurosis and ill conceived ideas, dear brother Jim stepped up to the plate and fulfilled his duties as a loving, caring son. He never asked for help nor queried as to why I was not as attentive as I had previously been in our lives. He just did what was needed always careful to give me updates when warranted. The day did, however, come when Jim actually called on me for support. The intense chemotherapy was reeking havoc on Mama's body. Her condition weakened her, and she was losing her ability to fight. After my conversation with Jim, I called her doctor to get his perspective. He concurred and suggested she needed something to spark her passions. He mused and offered his opinion that I find someone who could rouse her anger, as this might stimulate her will to live. Surely he jested. There was only one person born to fulfill this mission. Certainly it was me. I booked my flight.

I arrived in the evening after the Georgia sun had set. As I drove into her neighborhood, I recognized the old elementary school that was now serving as an administration building. There was familiarity in the small brick homes and family-owned businesses that lined the dimly lit streets. The air smelled of freshly cut grass while the pavement glistened from an early evening rain shower. Fear kept me in my car, circling her block for half-an-hour. Although I had no prior experience with the effects of chemotherapy, I knew enough to realize that her appearance most certainly would have changed. Would I be brave or would I fall apart? These queries kept me circling aimlessly through her small community looking for courage in the drooping oak trees, cracked sidewalks and misty fog that had now set in. Ultimately I found my courage, parked my car, and walked up the steps to her front door.

Mama had forgotten to turn on the porch light. I stood in the dark wrapped in my fears. After knocking vigorously on the large wooden door, I began to see lights popping up in the house. As each illumination appeared, I knew she drew nearer to the door. My heart pounded. The porch light quickly flashed on, and the turn of the old precision double lock penetrated the silence of the night. Mama cracked the door ever so slightly. The light from the living room highlighted the back of her head casting a shadow over her face. This simple illusion gave me a reprieve from an emotional reaction to anything I might have seen. Instead I was blessed with the opportunity to freely embrace her without caution or judgment. Her ribs protruded from her chest and the bones in her arms peeked through her thin, pale flesh as I pulled her body into mine. Her voice was weak, her hair was sparse, and her stance unsteady.

"Come on in, Honey," she said.

I loved it when she called me Honey. I followed her as she shuffled back to her room and the safety and security of her bed. As she rested against her pillow, I lay witness to the ravages of her chemical treatments. Her doctor was right. It was taking its toll on her.

For the remainder of that evening I compassionately listened to my mama as she expressed her pain, shared her sorrow, and unburdened her fears to me, as she had so often done in the past. I had become a master. I made a conscious decision to give her all the time she needed and wanted. She deserved it and had earned it. Before falling asleep that night, I am guessing she felt comforted knowing that I was home. The Prodigal Daughter had returned. My sleep, on the other hand, was restless and anxious. I lay in the darkness wondering what the following day would bring. How would I best serve her? Was I kind enough, generous enough, or patient enough? Had I grown less selfish? Could I step outside my self-centered fears and move into a place of compassion and empathy? I would know soon. While pondering these thoughts, I finally fell asleep.

With the dawn I was awakened by Mama's gentle moans and cries from her bed. It reminded me of those Saturday mornings when she jolted Jim and I from our deep teenage sleep with the Hoover vacuum cleaner. Although it was now more affable and somewhat benign on this particular morning I found it equally piercing to my ever-so-fragile sleep. I again made a conscious decision to allow her this day. A

The Garden of Eden

giveaway free day. A non-judgmental day. A day of complaints, angst, and bemoaning of her situation. I gave myself over to her freely. This time by conscious adult choice.

The first measure of my sincerity was the joy and ease with which I made her soft scrambled eggs and lightly toasted the Sunbeam white bread. I presented this scrumptious breakfast on the same tray she had used to serve Jim and me so many times when we were sick as children. Mama chose to cover the few prickly, fully gray hairs that remained with a soft blue knit cap. She rested her head against her pillow as I raised the hospital bed to a position more suitable for eating. I pulled my chair close to her, pushed the sterling silver fork into the eggs, and offered them to my weary patient. As she had so often done for us as children, I cupped my hand under her chin to catch any droppings that might fall from her mouth. Although she acknowledged that my morning menu was delicious, she was unable to eat more than a few bites.

For the rest of the morning, I sat by her side, intercepting phone calls from her First Baptist church friends, watching a television talk show from a local station with news from the Deep South, and idly conversing about my high school friends who had remained in our small hometown. Mid-morning she developed a slight fever. I dampened a wash cloth with cool water and placed it on her forehead. She lifted her fragile yet still beautiful hand and placed it on mine, as if to say, "Thank you, Daughter."

I could see the bright sun glistening through the windows as I sat in her darkened room. Mama had not been outside for some time now. What could be the most loving and kind gesture I might extend to her this day? I knew instantly what I needed to do. I helped her brush her teeth. I repositioned her soft blue cap to more fully cover those hair spikes on her head. I brushed a pale pink blush onto her cheeks and lowered the hospital bed so her feet easily touched the floor. I gathered her knit summer blanket around her and let her know that we were going for a ride. Eager to please me, she shuffled to the front door so weak she could hardly hold up her head.

I pulled open the door and the bright sun flooded the living room softly touching her face. Once on the porch she lost her resolve and became consumed by fear.

"I can't," she said with tears in her eyes as she grabbed my arm.

"Yes you can," I said grabbing her right back.

Instantly I began to see that anger her doctor had spoken to me about. She wanted to fight me and I knew it. There was a part of her that wanted to remain sick. That was her power over me. She would be sick—I would make her well. She would be sad—I would make her better. That was our dance. For now, I wanted to sit this one out. I knew that my will was stronger than hers at this moment, and I would have my way with her. She fought with all she had but was no match for me that day.

I wrapped her blanket tightly around her frail, feeble body, used my taut Los Angeles muscles, and picked up my mama and single-handedly carried her to my car. I rolled down the window, put a pillow on the floor to rest her feet, and gently placed her in the front seat. Away we went. I could see out of the corner of my eye a small hint of a smile forming on her left cheek. Did she let me win, or did I gain my victory honestly? I choose to believe that we both won. Our souls shifted that day and our journey together took a turn. Our dance now flowed, partners moving in unison.

We drove over the city streets and into the main business district of town. On our way we passed the old department store where she had purchased her Sunday bonnets on sale for all those years. I took her to the post office where she mailed a get well card to a friend. As we perused all the familiar sights of Albany, I rolled down the windows to let the breeze of our motion flow into the car. Mama turned her face to the side and allowed the wind to cool her chapped lips and the sun to bring light into her heart. I treated her to a vanilla frosty freeze cone at the local Dairy Queen. From there we drove to our favorite lake on Dawson Road where I pulled up under a shady ole oak tree and parked. Mama laid her head back and gave herself over to the day.

The sweet breeze, the soft sunlight, the quacking ducks, and the lapping of the water against the shore lulled her into a restful sleep. Now and again she would awaken, look over at me and smile, and then return to her sweet suspension of consciousness. I rested my hand against hers as we shared our afternoon together.

That evening I made dinner, served her as she sat upright in her bed, and turned the TV to a rerun of a Billy Graham Crusade. The Reverend's words and his impassioned pleas still touched her heart as though they were happening in real time. In his closing prayer Mama reached out her hand toward the screen as though making this gesture put her one step closer to the source. As the choir once again sang "Just As I Am," throngs of people filed down the stadium steps making their way to the stage to rededicate their lives to their Lord. Mama reached for her purse as she had done so many times in the past. She pulled out a five dollar bill and placed it in an envelope. I addressed it for her, put a stamp on the corner, and dropped it by the front door as an assurance that we would mail it the following day. I retired to my room, falling asleep easily knowing that we had had a good day. We did well together so now we could rest.

The following morning I was awakened by a clamoring coming from the kitchen. It was a sound reminiscent of those childhood days when Mama got into a cooking frenzy pulling pots and pans from the cabinets, opening and closing the refrigerator door, banging wooden spoons against glass bowls all the while humming one of her favorite Southern Baptist hymns under her breath. This was certainly an unexpected occurrence and one I was completely unprepared for experiencing this particular morning. I lay motionless, gazing at the stucco ceiling and hoping for silence.

Suddenly my olfactory organs were aroused with the smell of what I thought to be freshly cooked bacon causing me to sit upright in my bed. Was that other sound the sizzle of a farm-raised egg bubbling in the juice of that greasy bacon? My senses completely overtook me. I bolted out of my restful morning state and headed to the kitchen.

A Legacy *of Lies*

There was Mama, wig on head, spatula in one hand, and a homemade biscuit in the other looking for all the world to be the mama I had known and loved for so long. Without a good morning, or a how-did-you-sleep, she just looked me straight in the eyes.

"What are we doin' today?" she asked.

I was stunned, yet excited. What do mothers and daughters do together? I knew exactly what to say.

"We're going shopping. You need a new dress," I responded with glee.

Her face lit up like a klieg light and she let out a sweet, gentle chuckle with a hint of a smile. We sat down for our Southern breakfast along with a cup of freshly brewed coffee. Afterwards I drew a bath for her and helped her into the tub, something she had not enjoyed for some time. Afterwards, she put on her makeup, adjusted her wig, stepped into her high heels, grabbed her purse, and headed for the front door. Although she held onto the handrail, this time she took those stairs on her own without the aid of my taut LA muscles.

As we drove into town, the streets took on a brighter glow this day. We pulled into the parking lot of her favorite department store. Mama and I were about to embark on an adventure heretofore never attempted by us since my early childhood. We were going shopping, a task I loathe and generally participate in only out of necessity. It was deemed in my mind a "girly" thing, a side I rarely showed my mama. As we entered the Ladies department, I found a chair for her and had her take a seat. I combed the racks for outfits I thought she might be interested in and brought them to her for her approval. After some time, she made her choices and we headed for the dressing rooms. I helped her button, tie, or zip each of her selections. We looked into the mirror together and weighed the pros and cons of each. As I stood in that tiny dressing room, I was amazed at how far we had come. Never before in my wildest of dreams would I have ever envisioned Mama and me doing such a "girly" thing as shopping together. She reveled in every moment. I savored the experience as though sipping on a fine French wine. Ultimately Mama made her choice, and we left the store with two new outfits perfect for Sunday church.

We spent the next several days enjoying each other. We cooked together, visited her First Baptist friends, watched TV, and chatted about life. We even exchanged our views on world events, something we rarely agreed on. Although I would never have honestly shared my thoughts on world peace, nuclear warheads, a President with controversial policies, or homosexuality, I did carefully choose my words in an effort to maintain a certain level of civility between us. Perhaps she was doing the same, regardless, it worked, and no one left with egg on their face or scars in their heart.

I was to return to LA early on Sunday morning. I arose before the sun, dressed, finished packing, and prepared to leave on my journey back home. Mama, at the same time, also showered, put on one of her new outfits, donned a Sunday-go-to-meetin' hat and waved good bye to me as she headed for church for the first time in months. The tenuous, wispy woman I greeted only a week before was not the strong, stalwart woman who waved goodbye to me that beautiful Sunday morning. We were united yet independent women stronger for having been together.

On Monday of the following week she was to have further tests to determine the state of her cancer and what else might need to be done to move her forward toward wellness. Results were to follow on Wednesday. Mama and I spoke several times in those two days, the last as she prepared to leave for the doctor's office. We had previously shared our thoughts and prayers together. I tensely waited by the phone in my Los Angeles home. Later in the day, the call came through. I picked up the phone and could hear that Mama was softly crying. I thought the worst. When she finally did speak, in her sweetest of voices, she said, "It's gone." She was in remission. We cried and laughed until we were both exhausted. She would be able to continue her life and enjoy some of the things she had longed to do for so many years.

After that phone call, I reflected on what had happened and how we had arrived at that conversation. How did that frail, weakened, beaten-down body that opened the door only days before make such a miraculous comeback? The answer was clear to me. It was the power of love between a Mother and a daughter. There are none as deep, as complicated, as hurtful, as helpful, as nurturing, as damaging, as encouraging, as defeating, as loving, as despising nor as eternal. We can destroy this powerful phenomenon with the words and actions that we hurl carelessly at each other. Or, we can lift ourselves to the greatest heights conceivable to the human mind, body, and spirit. Mama and I had experienced the latter in those few days we shared together. When I was able to release my ego—expecting nothing in return—and allow selfless, untainted love to flow, we both had a victory. Mother in the body and child in the spirit. It was a miracle, one that we both agreed to and allowed to unfold before us.

Eleven

IT IS FINISHED

After my return to Los Angeles I resumed my busy schedule of work, Buddhist activities, clubbing on Santa Monica Boulevard, traveling around the country interviewing musical artists for radio shows, falling in love, tequila margaritas, cocaine on coffee tables, falling out of love, hot summer days at Venice Beach, long martini-filled lunches at the finest restaurants in LA, rollerblading, hikes up Mt. Wilson, Big Sur with the top down, passionate love affairs, lonely nights staring out my window overlooking the San Fernando Valley, chanting for hours, and encouraging countless Buddhist members to continue their individual quests for a better life for themselves and their families. It was a thrilling time filled with passion, angst, great challenges, yet equal rewards and multiple accomplishments.

As I continued my life, Mama also expanded hers. She fell in love and married her third and final husband. Her lifelong dream of a trip to

Europe came to fruition with him. She saw Buckingham Palace, the Eiffel Tower, the great cathedrals, the Mona Lisa, and the statue of David—things she had seen only in the pages of her favorite magazines and had longed to personally experience since her childhood days in Arlington, Georgia. Her new husband also bought her a mink stole and presented it to her on Christmas morning. She had only fantasized in her wildest of dreams that she and a mink stole would someday meet shoulder to shoulder. She proudly wore that furry ornament to Sunday church services every winter, starting in late September with the first hint of a cool breeze.

Winters departed into springs, springs into summers. Steamy summers drifted into falls that in turn shed their leaves and evolved into chilly winters once again. Four years passed as quickly as the brush of a summer breeze falling on a soft, delicate cheek. One afternoon as I was dashing about taking care of the work and home duties involved in my busy LA life, I received a phone call from my brother Jim. Mama's cancer had returned. This time there was no hesitation. There was no consideration for her age and frailty of body. It came at her with a vengefulness that instantly debilitated her and brought her to her knees, literally and figuratively.

Jim returned to his status as dutiful son. I resumed my previous "concern from afar" position as we all walked through this next phase together. Each of us wore our shields and played our parts with equal brilliance and inventiveness. Months of chemotherapy and radiation dragged on, each taking its physical and mental toll on Mama. She put on a fake brave face, yet with each treatment her will to fight diminished and her desire to remain on the planet lessened. I did not see her during this period although we spoke frequently. The holiday season was fast approaching. I contemplated my options and weighed my personal needs against the needs of my dear mama.

It was a sunny, fall day in Los Angeles. Life was full. The sky was blue, a brisk breeze ruffled the branches of the trees, red blossoms peeked out of the succulent Christmas cacti plants, and fluffy white

It Is Finished

clouds drifted by. My phone rang, penetrating the tranquility of the day. It was my brother, Jim. He said Mama's condition had become more complex. As a result, she was not responding to the treatment. He felt that if I wanted to see her, I had better head on home to Albany as soon as possible.

I set about changing my calendar, making phones calls, booking my flight, and dealing with all the eventualities of leaving town for an indefinite period of time. The flight from Los Angeles to Atlanta was uneventful yet made easier by the two Bloody Marys I enjoyed upon boarding. The glass of white wine with dinner, followed with a nice nap, made for a pleasant enough trip across the breathtaking skies and varied yet distinctive landscapes of our beautiful country. In Atlanta, I was to change planes to a smaller ten-seater for the forty-five minute flight to Albany.

Once in the air, strong storm clouds began to brew outside my window. The inconsequential aircraft was bantered about by the growing winds. Electrical shocks from the lightening lit the late afternoon sky. As we neared the Albany airport, the intensity of the clouds darkened, thunder claps rattled the wings, and the aircraft shook as though on a sea of raging waters. Nervousness began to overtake the other four passengers. The pilot subsequently announced we would be unable to land due to the dangers from the storm. As we circled the tiny airport, avoiding the strikes of lightening and rolls of thunder, I reflected on the ups and downs of my life with Mama. How odd it was that in these last moments of our time together, we once again, were unable to connect, kept apart by the wiles and beguiling behavior of Mother Nature. 'Round and 'round we spiraled in our insignificant orbit and endless loop of repetitive turbulent motion. I could see the ground below but was not yet able to touch it.

The more the storm raged, the more I became trapped inside my own mind. My heart longed to end this tumultuous journey and complete the mission laid out before me. Once I realized I could change my circumstances by changing my mind, the pilot announced over the PA system that we would be attempting a landing. Just as he was about to make his final approach with the runway lights lined up in front of us, a squall of a wind lifted the undersized plane up and off its course, aborting our landing. As though the pilot was now residing inside my head, with great determination, fearlessly and without hesitation, he attempted another landing forthwith. This time that same tempestuous wind seemed to softly lift us up and then ever so gently settle us down safely on the tarmac with nothing more than an amiable thud.

It had been awhile since I had seen Mama, so I was fearful once again of what I would find as I entered her room at Phoebe Putney Memorial Hospital. So long ago, my mama had welcomed me and my rosy cheeks into her world in this very place. I greeted my brothers, Clarence, Bill, and Jim along with their wives in the hallway outside her room. Jim took me aside and apprised me of her condition, suggesting that I might be shocked by what I saw. I recognized that I needed some time to compose my thoughts and emotions. I excused myself to the ladies room. As I leaned against the cold metal door, I asked God/Spirit/Buddha, to take me out of my self-absorbed world and allow me to be a vessel of compassion and Divine love for the one who needed it most, my mama.

No one could have prepared me for what I saw. My beautiful, kind, proud mama lay gaunt and motionless on the bed. Many of her front teeth were now missing. She could not have weighed more than 85 pounds, looking very much like a concentration camp survivor. When she saw me enter the room, she lifted her head from the pillow. We knew each other. A peace came over her face as she realized her only daughter was now safely back home. Her emaciated arms stretched out to welcome me once again. As I held her, I gently lifted the back of her nightgown to wipe my tears, still finding it challenging to allow my mama to witness my own vulnerability.

All her loving family gathered around her bed, as we spent the afternoon telling stories of our lives together and reminiscing about days gone by. Bill, often the jokester, shared a few funny tales while we

It Is Finished

roared with laughter. The air in the room was filled with the jubilance of joy and devotion. Mama seemed to wander in and out of consciousness yet appeared to be entertained by and revel in the love and care that her family was displaying toward her.

At the end of the evening, Mama became restless and impatient with her inability to communicate or make her needs known to us. Clarence made an effort to soothe her discomfort by breaking into one of her favorite Baptist hymns. How peaceful it must have been for her to hear the resonant tenor tones of her first born child lifting his voice in praise to God. In praise to her trusted Savior whom she believed with all her heart she was about to meet. She was going home. I climbed onto Mama's bed and tenderly lifted her fragile, skeletal body. I stretched my legs out on the bed and pulled her into my arms. I laid her back against my chest and rested her head on my shoulder. All her family now joined in song. "Softly And Tenderly, Jesus is Calling, Calling for you and for me." Our soft angel-voices and sweet melodious harmonies floated on gossamer wings above Mama's head. I wrapped my arms around her, delicately caressed her, and rocked her as though she was now *my* child. Our lives had come full circle.

As evening drew near, the Georgia sun began to set, signifying an end to a long day and possibly the end to a long and glorious life. One by one, Mama's family said their good-byes and left for home. No one offered to stay the night. Somehow we, the Gods, all of the universe knew and understood that I was the one for this night. Jim was the last to leave. I looked at him. He looked at me and with a silent empathetic agreement he stepped into the downward elevator. I stood in silence as the doors closed behind him. The sound of the swishing cables and the blast of hot air from the descending car blew through the crack of the closing doors and took with it my frightened breath. I stood for a few minutes in the busy hallway wondering what the night would hold for Mama and me.

I returned to her bedside where she lay sleeping. I spent the next hours quietly attending to her needs, offering a sip of water, a cube of crushed ice, a soft touch on her hairless head. The clamor of dinner dishes and the hushed voices of visitors leaving their loved ones for the night began to diminish. The quiet of the night set in. Ultimately I pulled my chair close to her bed, opened a magazine and lovingly rested my hand against hers. I could feel the pulse of her life blood slowly and almost softly flowing through her veins. We stayed this way for several hours. Occasionally a nurse would come in to check her vital signs and leave as quickly as she had arrived. I sat vigil remembering our life together and wondering how it was that in the beginning and in the end, it was just the two of us. In reality, no one actually helped us either time. She released me into this physical world, and I was releasing her into her longed-for spiritual world.

Somewhere around two o'clock in the morning, that same nurse came in to once again check her vital signs. This time she stopped. Mama's temperature had fallen to 94.7. This unnamed nurse walked over to my chair and took my hand.

"The hearing is the last thing to go. If there is anything you need to say to her, you should do it now," she said in a whisper.

This loving and gentle nurse had no way of knowing our history and yet she knew we needed to complete our circle. Once again, she left as quickly as she had entered.

I knew that this moment was coming and yet now that it was upon me, I felt lost. I felt fragile and without words. I moved to the end of Mama's bed and placed my hands on her tiny ankles. Our lives together flashed before me—all the joys, all the pain, all the hopes, the losses, the missed targets, all the needs, the longings, and all the unfulfilled dreams. I was completely overwhelmed by the magnitude of the moment. I wanted so to forgive. I wanted so to be forgiven. All the love, all the bruises, all the mysteries that lay before us and between us. I looked to the heavens and asked that God please help me. Help me make this a peaceful passage. Help me act honorably. Help me to act with dignity and without regret. I ran my hands along her legs.

"Mama ... Mama," I called her name.

It Is Finished

A name I had called so many times before. Tonight it was like no other. A tiny twitch on her cheek signaled that somewhere in her being she recognized my voice. Perhaps for a moment she too reflected back on all the times in our lives I had called her name. I rested my hands on her wrinkled, weary feet and gently massaged them, with a compassionate, comforting stroke. I knew she was waiting for me to speak. Through that touch and the sound of my voice we eternally connected in that moment.

"Mama, It's okay. Please don't worry. I will be okay. You can leave me now," I whispered with all the love in my heart.

I moved back to the side of the bed and once again placed my hand on hers. The hollow, haunting death rattle of her labored breath penetrated the stillness of that night. I sat and intently listened as she took each breath. Breathe in, breathe out, breathe in, breathe out, breathe in….and then there was silence. I waited. There was no more. It was finished. In an instant her spirit, her life force, her God nature had removed its Self and been scattered into the heavens. I imagined in that moment for her, God was opening the gates and welcoming her in.

"Welcome home, my good and faithful servant. You have done well."

She had now found her longed-for peace. I stood alone by her side. I tightly held my hand in hers. After a few, still, quiet moments I rang for the unnamed nurse.

As though she knew, Mama's nurse arrived quickly and walked to her side. She took her pulse and acknowledged with a nod that it was indeed finished. She offered her condolences and then began to remove Mama's jewelry. I extended my help. With shaking hands I struggled to release the snap on the gold bracelet Mama wore on her right wrist for many years. The nurse reached across the bed, placed her hands on mine, and together we released the tightened clasp. I embraced the golden treasure in my hands, carefully placing it in my side pants pocket.

It was now close to three o'clock. I made my first phone call to my brother, Jim. He quickly picked up following one ring, as though he had been lying by the phone waiting for the call.

"Is she gone?" he asked.

"Yes." I said.

Several days later, our family and Mama's friends all gathered to honor her and celebrate her life. A life well-lived and one filled with accomplishments. The funeral home was packed to capacity. I was most certainly still in shock and haunted by the memory of her recent passing. I do, however, recall the pastor's words and the gentle, kind way he spoke of her. He focused his thoughts on my mama's hands, referring to them as strong hands, working hands, giving hands, and loving hands.

I thought as I sat there, knowing many eyes were upon me, that this was one of those mystical moments. One of those shared karmic, transcendental unworldly events. Having never met this pastor, certainly he was not privy to the importance that hands had played in my life with Mama. Our first meeting as I entered this world when she took my tiny hand in hers on her birthday so long ago was our beginning. Then there was the long walk on my first day of school when she held and then released my hand to my first grade teacher opening a world of wonder and knowledge that lasted a lifetime. Later and equally as profound I recalled the day she grabbed my hand away from Granddaddy's and then released it just as quickly. This too opened a world of wonder, knowledge, and self-exploration that has lasted a lifetime. And our most recent exchange as I held her hand while she breathed her last breath in this lifetime, releasing her to a more profound world. God's world of wonder, knowledge, exploration, and more lifetimes. It was a befitting spoken end to our mysterious and visionary life together.

Following the ceremony, as is the tradition, our cars lined up behind the flower draped hearse preparing to make the final journey to her resting place in the Crown Hill Cemetery on Dawson Road. I traveled with my family in the limousine directly behind Mama. The procession was led by a handsome police officer on a white Harley Davidson motorcycle. At each intersection, this young officer, with his

It Is Finished

cap over his heart, stopped all traffic from the four corners allowing Mama's cortege to move without incident. All cars pulled to the side of the road while the occupants placed their hands over their hearts and bowed their heads as we passed. I thought it most appropriate that the world took time to honor, acknowledge, and pay deference to the life of my mama. For one brief moment their world stopped as mine did that chilly December morning.

The graveside ceremony was held in a tiny chapel near the crypt where Mama had asked to be placed. As we entered, I glanced across the cemetery to the towering pine tree that shaded my beloved daddy's resting place. Now they were both gone and perhaps together again. Mama's decision to be buried with her last husband was befitting to and honoring of her Southern values to the end. I had always envisioned Mama taking her place beside Daddy under that pine tree. Her choice brought me no comfort even though I knew it was hers to make. I was awestruck by the knowledge that even now, Mama and I had our differences of opinion. Death does not change one's karma. Instead it perhaps adds to it and provides more opportunity for growth, understanding, compassion, and healing. I was tempted to go against her wishes for a moment. Wisdom prevailed, and I allowed myself to respect my mama enough to honor the decision she had made for "her eternity." I was at peace.

Following the sweet service, the pastor led us in a closing prayer, and we headed back to Mama's place. As was the Southern tradition, the house was filled with potted plants, chrysanthemums, and fragrant fresh flowers. The kitchen was bustling with her First Baptist Church friends, although they were much older now, their hearts were still young and brimming with love and concern for our family. The aroma of crisply cooked fried chicken, fresh butterbeans, and homegrown tomatoes floated through the doorways, out into the halls, and into each room of the house. There was, of course, an abundance of sweet iced-tea. Her house was filled with laughter, condolences, and heavy hearts, yet joy in the knowledge that Mama was now at peace.

Her body was whole once again and she was free from her sorrows. I was comforted by the presence of those who loved and respected her. It was a day of deep sadness and one of great joy. Once again I was asked to hold both with equal weight and balance.

In the following days, her friends left to their quiet lives, my family returned to their homes, and I was once again left alone with Mama. Just the two of us deciding what remained and what did not. My most painful experience came one afternoon as I went through Mama's personal clothing. As I stood in her closet amongst her "homemade" Sunday hats for all seasons, her most prized mink stole, and her best *goin'-to-meetin'* outfits, my nostrils filled with the scent that was uniquely Mama. I was overcome with grief. How had a life so well-lived come down to these textile fibers of cotton, hand-woven wool, and manmade polyester? All these garments that had so much meaning in her life that now had none to anyone but me. I sat on the floor beside her well-traveled high heels and wept for the first time.

The following day I called the Salvation Army, an organization that Mama approved of and believed to be a doer of good works. I carefully packed every dress, pant suit, winter coat, skirt, sweater, pair of shoes, and special Sunday hat, holding each to my heart before I put it away for good. With deep sorrow I drove these precious, meaningful, and seemingly relevant articles of clothing to their donation center on Oglethorpe Boulevard.

The people receiving these remains of a life knew nothing of her struggles, her loves, her disappointments, her joys, her achievements, her defeats, her longings, or her fulfillments. They made no inquiries as to the reasons why nor did they ask about the who. They simply did their job, helped me unload the car, took the bags from me, wrote out a receipt, and with an uncaring smile thanked me for my donation as they had done so many times before. I walked away with a white piece of paper that might be used as a tax deduction for someone. All that living, four births, three husbands, grandchildren, jobs, homes, Saturday mornings, church services, paychecks, tears, and

It Is Finished

laughter—all found in a receipt from the Salvation Army. I did, however, take great comfort in knowing that perhaps a number of women in my small hometown of Albany, Georgia, would now don those textile fabrics and Mama would live on in them.

The next few days I packed up her silverware, china, her hand painted tea cups and pitcher, all those things that she had deemed special to her. I shipped some of them to my home in Los Angeles and held out others for my siblings and their children. During the course of her later years, Mama opened up her house to her children, grandchildren, and loved ones. It was first come, first served with her. Whatever you wanted you simply had to ask. She kept a running tab in an eight-by-ten spiral notebook where she recorded each request in her own handwriting. This was essentially her will, and we all honored its contents in the end. The majority of Mama's household belongings were to be placed in an estate sale with the proceeds divided amongst her four children. The house that Jim and I grew up in on 8th Avenue was to be sold and divided amongst her four birthed children and the two children that my daddy had fathered by his first wife. Mama was generous in death as she had been in life.

It was a challenging week for me, yet on some level I went into automatic mode, performing my duties and responsibilities as her only daughter. I was happy to complete my tasks and return to my busy and full life in Los Angeles. The seeming safety of my familiar and comfortable style of living was not without a price. Sleep regularly escaped me. For the year following Mama's death I relived our last night together, heard that final breathe in, and recalled her frail and fragile body in its ending moments. I did finally seek some professional help in moving past that haunting memory. Life would go on.

Twelve

REVELATIONS AT LAST

Even after all these years, it is still difficult to recall the events of my last hours with our mama. During those days Jim and I united and more deeply bonded, showing mutual respect for each other. Now here we stand at this moment with a very large schism between us. It is two days since my arrival in Nashville, and I still have trepidations about pursuing Jim's request for evidence. I cannot seem to let my history go. There must be secrets in those events that will assist me in moving forward from here. I go back in time to the days when I was still raw and broken open from her loss.

It was several months after I returned home to Los Angeles when I received a check in the mail for my share of Mama's estate. I had previously made a decision to leave Billboard Magazine to begin my own small inflight entertainment business. My inheritance provided me with the means to purchase the equipment I needed and to turn my garage into a recording studio. With each nail that went into the walls, each window carefully placed in a new opening, each stroke of the paint brush, each palette of carpeting laid, I thought of Mama. The final result was exactly as I had envisioned it. I began to accumulate a number of long term, loyal clients. Although I spent most of Mama's money on this business endeavor, it turned out that it was a gift that just kept on giving for the next twenty years as a result of my humble yet mighty garage production company. Mama lived on in so many ways.

As I grew more deeply in my Buddhist faith and continued my self-exploration, my drug use decreased. I do, however, recall my final cocaine binge quite vividly. I had gained access to some potent "happy dust" on a Wednesday afternoon from a friend. We did a couple of lines and headed to Venice Beach for a late lunch. That night we did more coke, put the top down on the Volkswagen Rabbit Convertible, and headed to Santa Monica Boulevard, and the clubs. It was a night of snorting in the bathroom, in the back seat of the car, and in the IHOP on the Boulevard in West Hollywood. After returning home around four o'clock in the morning, there was no sleep to be had—just wild, crazy sex intensified by the chilled Chardonnay we shared 'til dawn.

I tooted and drank for the next four days without once closing my eyes for sleep. Finally on Sunday, I unplugged my phone, pulled down the shades, fell into my bed and slept for 24-hours knowing that the Sabbath was indeed a day of rest. When I awoke on Monday morning every inch of my body screamed in pain. My teeth throbbed. The inside of my ear canals pounded. My eyes, I am certain, resembled ten pound paper weights. My stomach churned like a cement mixer at a construction site. The muscles in between my toes ached. The hair on my head was so sensitive to the touch I was unable to rest it on my pillow. Light creeping through the cracks in the window sills shocked my fragile brain, sending it into excruciating spasms. I will never forget how my body felt that day. And most certainly I will never forget the deep, most morose, suicidal thoughts that invaded my mind as I attempted to cope with the effects of a gluttonous drug feast of such magnitude. Although I did not consciously make a determination to give up drugs, somehow my life, my higher Self, my God nature knew that the gig was up. My body was too toxic from use and misuse of the powdery substance. It was screaming back at me.

The law of physics does suggest that a void is ceremoniously filled as it appears. These vacuums in the universe have a natural ebb and flow to them. One opens up, another is filled. Although alcohol had always been my drug of choice, it now became my only drug of choice filling to capacity the void left by the intoxicating and dangerous nose candy.

As I moved forward, I became more aware that long-term romantic relationships continued to elude me. In my quiet time and personal moments I allowed myself to fantasize and envision more intimacy in my life. I had learned that in order to bring forth a result one must take some form of action. That being said, I was also aware that clubbing, drinking, and casual sex were not the appropriate actions to bring about the much longed for deeper relationships. I determined to be stricter and less serendipitous with my causes.

As in my Southern Baptist faith and many other religions, Buddhism held a dimly lit view of homosexuality. It was strongly suggested that those of us who dwelt in this world might migrate into the more accepted world of heterosexuality. It was presented as though it might be as effortless as changing from one lane to another on the Hollywood Freeway. Those passing down this edict never took into consideration what happens on that same freeway during rush hour traffic on any given day. Anyone who travels them knows that nothing happens. There is no changing from lane to lane. There is no movement. There is simply waiting.

Regardless of this knowledge, I made several poor attempts at relocating my sexual world with the most dismal of results. My paralyzing need to please led me to sexual encounters in which I found myself staring at the ceiling as my "partner" pleasured himself. A most familiar means of escape from a difficult and damaging experience. I had been there so many times before. The only difference was that I was now numb and devoid of all feeling. The full effects of handing my power over to Mama that night when Daddy left us and the unwanted liaisons with Granddaddy were fully felt within each of these hollow rendezvous.

In the most perplexing and unorthodox ways, Mama's hold on me remained substantial and constant. None of it was conscious. Yet my behavior, my inner actions with others, the lack of intimacy in my relationships, and the deep, melancholy I carried in my bones illustrated daily the constraints that this hold hung 'round my soul. The grip of my despair was so powerful I often contemplated suicide.

I could hear Mama's voice whispering words of displeasure in my ears. On occasion, I was certain she had temporarily taken over my body. She was speaking as me, functioning as me, and still living her life through me. Parallel to this, on occasion I found myself whispering words of love, posing questions of concern, offering expressions of joy for an accomplishment, or sharing a moment of adventure with that part of me that was still her. She was me. I was her. We were a shared being, still looking to be made whole by the other. And yet to the outside world, the glass house in which I lived appeared to be freshly polished, beautifully reflective and solid in structure. These feelings followed me and even with Mama firmly ensconced, I made it through those failed sometimes aborted, illicit sexual affairs.

One afternoon I returned home from work to find on my doorstep a single pink carnation neatly tied with a matching ribbon in a clear glass vase. The accompanying hand written note simply read, "I hope you have a great day." I was touched and wondered who might have been so thoughtful and went about my evening. Several days later I returned home from work to find another single carnation, with matching ribbon in a clear vase. This time the color was red. The hand written note said, "Have a nice weekend." Now my curiosity was definitely tweaked. No one claimed responsibility for the floral benevolence.

Weeks passed. Without rhyme or reason, on no particular day the single carnations appeared on my doorstep. Each was accompanied with a simple handwritten note affirming goodwill, good times, or good thoughts for me. I began to find that my ride home through the streets of Los Angeles was somehow more interesting. I experienced a sense of excitement rather than frustration as I crawled through the slow moving traffic on Los Feliz Boulevard. My thoughts wandered to my doorstep. I envisioned jumping out of my car, opening the gate to my front yard, walking over the cracks in my sidewalk, past the freshly planted daisies, the blossoming grapefruit tree, and onto the steps of my home. Would I find a flower there? If so, what color would it be? What would the note say today? Would it hold any clues previously unnoticed? More time passed. My mysterious bearer of gifts and unknown admirer remained just that, unknown.

Several more months passed and one day after another fun-filled ride home from work, I arrived safely at my quaint cottage on Division Street. As I pulled into the driveway I noticed an unfamiliar car parked near the curb. I gave it no thought other than perhaps a neighbor had a visitor. I unloaded my car. As I opened the creaky, age-worn wooden gate leading to my front porch, I looked up to find a handsome, blushing, blond man standing by my blooming daisy bushes. The startled look on his face let me know I had inadvertently run face to face with my mystery admirer and bringer of flowers. He was not a stranger to me as he was a familiar face in the Buddhist organization, one I had known for years. This fact, however, did not minimize my level of shock that my conundrum had now been solved. The charade was over.

He was not tall, dark and handsome as the fairy tales insist. He was simply tall, very light, very blonde, and beyond seriously handsome. My astonishment was experienced on two levels. One, he was of the male persuasion. I had surmised over those long months of surprise and anticipation that anyone who was that thoughtful, caring, and romantic must surely be of the feminine gender. My second layer of dismay was found in the realization that someone as charming, handsome, and charismatic as my enigmatic "stranger" would be interested in pursuing me for any purpose. I was wrong on both counts.

To the unenlightened eye our simple encounter amongst the daisies that day may have appeared innocent and perhaps inconsequential. To the illuminated one, that rendezvous was the cause that altered the course of my journey and set me onto an unexpected, unpredictable, and impetuous ride.

I did not leap with gusto nor with any sense of ease onto that great heterosexual Freeway of Love. It had been years since I had spent an evening alone with a gentleman paramour. I was instead, cautious and filled with fear. Months passed. At long last my handsome suitor and I agreed to a Sunday afternoon movie in Santa Monica with dinner to follow near the beach. Good conversation enhanced by chilled French champagne, lobster tails, and a dry bottle of Chardonnay made for a lovely though intoxicating evening.

Many such encounters would follow. Enchantment, exotic wines, shared beliefs, affection and more lovely champagnes were the perfect nutrients for the gestation period of our romance. It did indeed blossom, and one evening I found myself moments away from lying on my bed about to share a carnal connection with my alluring admirer. This was an impending event I had feared yet knew would one day appear. And yet somehow, it seemed right and good and perfect that we would find ourselves in that quiet, loving, and generous place. Although we both knew my sexual history, this common knowledge did not allow hesitancy, reluctance, or a wavering second for either of us. The softness of his smooth white skin and the tender, gentle way in which he caressed by body clothed me in a cloak of safety and sweet sanctuary. I surrendered completely to the exchange of feelings, to the pulsating, wanton passion and the grace of allowing my body to be touched with simplicity, care, and authentic gentleness.

The following morning I opened my eyes to see the slim, almost delicate body of my handsome, blond suitor lying next to me. As I watched the minute sliver of sunlight cascading across his out stretched hand, I knew my life had changed in a profound way. No longer were we casual participants in a weekend romance. No matter how much we would care to deny, minimize, or eliminate it, sex does change everything. With one seemingly simple act, we had shifted from the casual to the profound. Our lives together would grow from there.

Over the coming months and year, our relationship ebbed and flowed reflecting the changing tides of the pulsating Pacific Ocean where we shared so many evenings. He had been the product of a broken home. I clearly saw and understood his wounds. In so many ways, we matched. Where I had a weakness, he injected one of his strengths. I reciprocated. My strengths filled in where his weaknesses lay. I fell deeply in love with him. Over time, it became clear to both of us that we did not want to live apart but would chose to share our lives together. He asked me to marry him. I gleefully accepted.

We were married one stormy October evening sharing our joy with four-hundred of our closest friends and family. I knew that this was an event that Mama had prayed about and longed for since she first laid eyes on my rosy, red cheeks as we began our life together. Physically, of course, she was not present. Yet she most certainly made sure that she was there in Spirit and that she was in a conspicuous position.

We had placed a chair beside us for one of the speakers who was to bless our marriage. He was delayed by the rain and was not present when the ceremony began, therefore, that chair remained "empty" throughout the service. Had I thought about it previously, I would have set aside a place in her honor, however, since it had not occurred to me, she simply took control of matters and provided her own, fully positioned and close up view of our nuptials. As she was wont to do when excited, I could hear her voice in its higher octaves.

"If you think for one minute I am going to miss this event, you are out of your mind."

Revelations at Last

I knew exactly what had happened and who was sitting in that "empty" chair.

It was truly a glorious and most inspiring occasion. As the doors swung open to the perfect swell of the music, and I walked through on the arm of my brother Jim in a traditional long hooped white gown, our guests stood en masse and cheered. I thought perhaps most of them believed it was a mighty damn long time coming. There were others who just simply felt relieved that it actually happened. We shared a most romantic and intoxicating honeymoon through California's wine country and up the Pacific coast to Big Sur. I was mostly out of my mind with love, joy, and contentment. I was a married woman.

In all my preparations for the wedding and the events leading up to it, I had forgotten to imagine, envision, plan, or even remotely think about what life would be like after the festivities. Although we did spend some happy months in honeymoon bliss and sexual ecstasy, soon the cracks of our frail, foundationless marriage began to shatter our euphoric nuptials. Alcohol became the glue that I consciously and carefully placed in each cavern of disappointment I felt and witnessed in our relationship. More did not make better. Less was untenable.

Words were not spoken, voices were not raised, fists were not clutched, fears were not shared. Silently we breathed the same air, consumed the same food, practiced our Buddhist faith, rested in the same bed. We negotiated parallel paths while each step took us in equally diverse directions. Quietly and inwardly my heart began to break. Alcohol soothed the wounds.

We struggled. I struggled. He struggled. I drank. He drank. Completely overcome by the pain I felt, I decided to give it up and eliminated alcohol from my daily routine. I did well for four months. Then one night my husband and I had an argument, a simple and uneventful one at best. He easily and peacefully fell asleep in our bed. After hearing his soft, familiar sleep noise, I carefully lifted the covers off my body, placed my bare feet onto the hardwood floor and with great care walked into the kitchen. Without thought or concern, I opened the liquor cabinet, grabbed the Courvoisier bottle, poured an eight ounce glass, and drank it down without a breath. I remember dropping my head back, looking up at the ceiling as though in a prayer and feeling for the first time in four months, peace.

A fluid tryst in the dark of my kitchen after midnight proved equal to an atomic explosion in a hill of fire ants or a cascading avalanche onto a lone skier high in the Alps. This time there was no way out. I was completely and unabashedly consumed by my liquid elixir. For the first time in my long life as a consumer, I was no longer a "functioning alcoholic." I was unable to navigate through my daily life except for the minimal tasks required of any adult.

My husband's business often required that he leave for work as early as 5:30 AM. Most mornings I was enjoying a cold Beck's Beer by 7:30. He and I had grown so far apart he did not notice that his wife was being buried alive in his own home.

My unhealthy thoughts and tortured feelings ignited my personal inferno. My life became a living hell. Alcohol doused the flames. The remaining smoldering smoke was tolerable. However, as with any fire, under the quiet of the white smoke, hot, red sparks lie in waiting. They were waiting for the ideal circumstances. A slight shift of the wind, a stray thought, a desperate moment. Alcohol exacerbated and further lacerated my wounds. The sparks reignited. The flames once again erupted and billowed through my mind, body, and spirit. I could no longer live inside my tormented being. Suicide was a daily option.

In Los Angeles, Cinco de Mayo, May 5, is a day set aside to celebrate the Mexican victory over the French in the "Batalla de Puebla" symbolizing unity and patriotism for the Hispanic community. It is marked by dancing in the streets, tequila flowing from lush fountains, and fresh tamales offered in crowded sidewalk cafes. As this particular day of festivities began, I opened a bottle of cold Heineken beer poured it into a chilled, frosty mug, and sat down to enjoy the penetrating sounds of mariachis meandering around and through the thick smog of the Southern California morning. So as not to miss out on the celebrations of the day, at nine o'clock in the morning I switched to Cuervo Gold tequila. It was not long before I found that sweet, familiar place of temporary peace. Out of this contentment emerges the persistent, nagging thought that takes over the alcoholic's mind, "If I feel this good, then how much better will I feel with more?" With that I switched to Brandy and Coke, my husband's favorite drink. I danced about naked in our living room happily singing and humming aloud. Freedom abounded. Cares forgotten. Pains masked.

Time passed. Deep inside that tranquility, fun, and peace, lying in wait is a hazardous, unpredictable and often lethal domain. It is as though the-enemy-within turns and begins to devour itself. Frivolity phased into melancholy. Song transposed into self-directed rage. Dancing feet collapsed in despondency and despair. Mariachis morphed into madness. This is the living definition of insanity.

I recall searching for the brandy bottle as I stumbled about. I raised it above my head and began to pour the poison over my face screaming as loud as I could without throwing up.

"Go ahead you Motherfucker. Kill me. Kill meeeee."

I just wanted to find a way out. Just get me a way out of my life. Get me a way out of this living hell. I spun around again and again. Exhausted, I simply and quietly crumpled to the floor. For how long, I do not know. I was awakened by the sound of my answering machine blaring out my personal, upbeat greeting with the obligatory request for my caller to leave a message. In a semi-conscious state, I noticed that my head rested in a pool of my own vomit. In the distance, I heard the sweet, melodious voice of my dear friend Y.

"I haven't heard from you in a few days. Are you alright?" she said as a concerned "sister."

I heard her and yet I waited. I thought about the consequences of my next action. Was I willing to be exposed? Was I willing to allow myself to be vulnerable? With great hesitancy I crawled to the phone. I picked it up.

"No, I am not okay" I slurred back to my confidant and well-wisher.

I could say no more. Y quickly read my despair. She sensed the fragility of my life at that moment and took my cry for help with grave seriousness. My memory of the impending events is hazed by the alcohol. I do know with all that is within me that her actions were swift and consequential. With multiple phone calls she had secured a place for me in the rehabilitation facility of the Kaiser Permanente Hospital on Sunset Boulevard.

The next few moments hold my biggest regret and my greatest blessing. Y was unable to leave her work to accompany me. I never thought to call a taxicab. Instead, I elected to drive myself. As I turned the key in the ignition and placed my car in reverse, I was conscious and aware enough to look to the heavens. I called forth all the Gods and Goddesses within the Universe to protect me and all those on the road with me as I traveled through the streets of Los Angeles to my new beginning.

I left no note for my husband as to my whereabouts. I walked out of our house without a trace. I recall nothing about that journey. To this day I do not know where I parked my car. I do know that I am grateful every moment of my life that no one was harmed that day by my reckless and self indulgent behavior.

After arriving at Kaiser, I recall lying on my back in the examination room looking up at the fluorescent lights as they flickered and spun above my head. After much questioning and probing, I was deemed more than fit for rehab. A cab was called to transport me to their detox facility in Carson, California. With true alcoholic ethics, I manipulated the cab driver into making a detour off the 10 Freeway with the guise of calling my husband. This was a call I had no intention of making. We stopped at a 7/11 convenience store. I purchased a tall can of Budweiser and headed back to the cab with a small brown bag. I lifted that frosty, receptacle of bubbly sedation in celebration of Cinco de Mayo, 1993, as we wove through the rush hour traffic that sunny afternoon.

The Wedding.

Thirteen

THE OMEGA BECOMES THE ALPHA

Detox is a world unto itself. Visualize if you will, a red brick building filled with alcoholics and addicts wandering about in various stages of drunkenness or intoxication from some exotic drug or another. While residing here one is not expected to eat, sleep, sit, stand, speak, or even think. There are only two requirements that must be met. Each participant must refrain from partaking of any controlled substance through any and all orifices. Believe me when I say that there were people there who would have shoved a vile of coke into any open aperture found anywhere on their bodies. Secondly, all occupants, willing or unwilling, must attend three Alcoholics Anonymous or Narcotics Anonymous meetings each day.

Imagine hanging over a toilet bowl throwing up from the bottom of your toes. You are chilled to the bone from the poisons leaving your body. You have absolutely no ability to form words or put sentences together. While weak in the knees, and unable to stand from the debilitating effects of going cold turkey, crazy thoughts are running rampant through your mind. You have a headache so massive you can feel the blood pulsing in, around, and through each cavern of your brain. There are no excuses accepted. *All* must march, crawl, or otherwise be dragged to the meeting room. To the outside viewer we must have resembled the unique array of characters in "One Flew over the Cuckoo's Nest." I would have to say that our Nurse Ratched turned out to be whoever dragged us or wrapped us in our "blankies" kicking and screaming to all those unwanted, unheard, and uncared about meetings. Although it is somewhat foggy now, I did survive the ordeal.

Following my two-week stay in the Detox Hotel from Hell, I was moved directly to a mental facility. I was declared at risk for administering personal bodily harm. That's detox talk for, I was suicidal. Stripped of all the masks that camouflaged my feelings, I was an exposed, raw nerve. In many ways, alcohol had protected me. In a most peculiar and idiosyncratic way, it had kept me alive all those years. The many reasons why I drank were now un-shrouded. Exposed as the true lies that they were.

I stayed confined within those four walls for a month. Secrets were brandished, rage was discharged, sorrow spewed, regrets abounded. All fell upon the deaf ears of those faded non-descript beige walls. There was a sense that I had not been the first to so take advantage of, exploit, and abuse them. Upon my release from the mental health facility, I began a six-week out-patient recovery program. In protest of nothing and in support of all things, I downsized my long brown, curly locks to a half inch buzz cut. Although I did quite well in the program, my advisor thought it would be wise for me to "re-enlist" in an effort to assist me in fully grasping the tenets of the course. In other words, she felt I needed to understand more deeply what it means to be a raging alcoholic/addict. I followed her direction and re-enrolled.

Upon returning home after my long and arduous pilgrimage, I was overcome with fear as I approached my front door. So much had happened since last I drove away in my drunken stupor that Cinco de

Mayo day. In a state of panic, I called my dear friend K and asked if she would help me walk through this first journey home. She left for my house instantly.

I made it into my living room overwhelmed with an enormity of feelings as I saw our home in disarray and chaos. Almost two months without my care had taken a toll on my busy husband and our surroundings. As a human being, I felt depleted on all levels. Mentally, physically, emotionally and most certainly spiritually. I had nothing left. So weakened by my condition, I could no longer stand in my body. I had not an ounce of energy to be present for myself. I was an empty, diminished woman. I collapsed face down on our living room floor and stretched out my arms as though attempting to grasp and hold to myself some form of life. Something to fill me up. Anything to save me.

K arrived. Almost anyone else might have questioned or commented on my circumstances. Not my dear K. She quietly observed me for a moment. Then without hesitation and without words, she knelt down beside me. Ever so carefully she unfolded her body on top of mine. She pressed her warm breasts against my back, stretched her arms out placing them gently onto mine and inter-twined our fingers, encircling my fragile being. She breathed into me. Her unconditional love fused into my bankrupt soul. She engulfed me with compassion and unfailing support. I will never forget the peace of knowing that someone so deeply cared about me. That love allowed me for the first time to believe that there would be a brighter day. That I would not only survive but thrive as I moved forward in my newly sober life. I knew I was privileged and profoundly blessed.

As I progressed, it became clear to me that recovery doesn't have an end date. It isn't finished by the close of summer or the start of spring. It is on-going, life-long, in-your-face, lurking behind every negative thought or feeling. It must be nurtured each day as a newly planted garden. There are many guidelines, yet each person must negotiate and blaze their own path. It is a challenge everyday. You have to want it more than anything else in your life at the time. I scratched my way out of the pits of hell simply to breathe each day.

My marriage took a big hit. When one partner changes the rules of engagement in order to survive, the other partner is left with some difficult choices. They may choose to join in by incorporating similar changes into their half of the relationship. They may choose to remain the same and absorb the consequences. Or as I see it, the final option, they may choose to walk away. We tried, we talked, we read, we prayed, we cried, we "therapied" ourselves into exhaustion. Ultimately we both realized in an instant that although the love was big, the schisms between us were even grander. We would walk away from each other. I with a broken heart. He into another marriage. Sometimes love may not be enough.

I understood that too many demons had their stakes in me. I knew I had to take control and heal myself from the inside out. I had to walk my journey alone in order to ever be whole and complete as a woman. I began a profound period of therapy, study, self-examination, meditation, yoga, prayer, Chinese herbs, group therapy, AA meetings, NA meetings, CODA meetings, and Women for Sobriety meetings. I was supported by the love, grace and forgiveness of my family and friends. I ultimately returned to college and received my Master's Degree in Psychology. I was a driven woman.

As children we have an innocence and purity in our understanding of life. We are drug and alcohol free so our thinking is clear. For me, this clarity ended at sixteen in my sister's Lincoln Continental on the Jersey Shore with my first taste of vodka and orange juice. I am convinced I was an alcoholic from that first drink forward. I nurtured and cajoled it until I took my last sip of Budweiser in the back seat of that cab on the way to rehab. Only with sobriety did clarity return.

While on my path of abstinence and decipherability, I was stunned and astonished by the rage I unleashed toward my granddaddy as I relived the abuses again and again. I was introduced to Core Energetics Therapy. Here a safe environment was created to release and absorb my fury. In this method, it is believed that we hold all the traumas we have experienced in our bodies. They lie there quietly on a cellular level. Every time we clinch a muscle or take a deep breathe out of fear, that energy is caught and held somewhere in our body until we tap it and allow it to be freed. My rage had been lying dormant, sheltered, and impregnable behind my cavalcade of sex, drugs, alcohol, and personal responsibilities. It was beyond painful to dig so deep inside to excavate and expose malignant cancers that had been growing there since early childhood. There were times when the search was so dark I could feel sharp-nailed claws digging into the flesh of my wounded soul, tearing out the cancerous incubus at its roots. It was an arduous task, one that took guts and courage. It was painful, frightening, exhilarating and mystical all at the same time. It took a ravenous commitment, an unwavering desire and a profound capacity to tolerate anguish.

I peeled away the darkness one layer at a time. One experience led into another into another, into another, each awakening a slim glimmer of hope. I came to recognize that all the deep breaths and clinched muscles I used to brace myself for Granddaddy's onslaught were trapped somewhere inside me. Each needed to be tapped. Each needed to be healed. Each release brought tears and more clarity. I would walk a little taller. I would open a little more. Years passed.

Sometimes, even with all my effort, I felt like I was back at zero. Suicidal thoughts would once again emerge. Incompetency abounded in my mind. Self-worth was nonexistent. I longed to soothe my angst with a Margarita or a shot of gin. It would have been so easy to calm those demon thoughts. Just a little something to take the edge off. All that *"stinkin' thinkin'"* ran rampant through my brain like a broken eight-track audio tape. Over and over and over. Some days were torture. Some minutes were torture. Some seconds were torture.

It was a daily struggle. Yet somehow in those moments, I would again find the inner strength to begin anew. I'd call my AA sponsor, get to a meeting, or take a hike in the Santa Monica Mountains. And

The Omega Becomes the Alpha

I would always go back to therapy. Back to digging. Back to raw exposure. One day at a time, sometimes, one moment at a time.

One afternoon while in a session, I was stunned to feel a connection to something that was beyond me. It was so much greater and more profound than me. It was so much more encompassing and whole and gentle and wise and good. It was something I had never felt before. I reached inside to those gaping, empty spaces asking God for peace and healing. Suddenly a pure white light entered the room cascading from above, showering me with its mesmerizing beauty. I was almost blinded by its brightness, and yet it was soft and gentle. I felt weightless and lifted from the room. Tears began to effortlessly flow, streaming down my face. I completely gave into my ethereal experience. I permitted the beauty of the light to shatter the wounds of my heart. It appeared to burst through my psyche leaving me with a feeling of rapture and a wave of great joy. It was an out of body experience that I actually experienced consciously within my body. It was a holy liberation.

As I reveled in this grand and glorious release, the other members of my group gently laid their hands on me. Others stroked my hair. I was fully embraced by their love and compassion. While in this euphoric state, I found the gift I had searched for the entirety of my life. It was not wrapped in gold paper nor was it adorned with a lovely bow of satin ribbon. It came simply, without pretense or fanfare. The longed-for gift I found was forgiveness. It flowed into my heart, into my being, into the very breath of my life. With new eyes of absolution, I then looked into the tortured, tormented soul of my granddaddy, my own mama's father, and I wept. I wept for him. I wept for his suffering. For his torment. For his demons—demons surely far greater than my own. I wept and for the first time, I forgave.

With this as my inspiration in the following years, I traveled many roads, climbed multiple mountains, coasted through voluminous valleys, walked alone, ran arm-in-arm, discovered many and gained much. I came to see that there were no saviors on white horses. There was me. Woman becoming stronger and wiser. Woman standing taller. Woman surrounded by her tribe of *Sistahs* also standing taller. And woman finding grace, healing her Self one august demon at a time.

Healing is a life-long journey and although I had made great progress, there was still my most ambitious peak to master, the gauntlet most Herculean to maneuver, the voyage most challenging to pilot. It was most certainly my relationship with Mama. Yes, there was rage lying in wait there as with Granddaddy. I came to see that this kind of madness can be violent and without controls. It is volatile in its nature and without redemption. It is volcanic and as such it indiscriminately spews its thunderous, scorching lava upon all those in its path. Ultimately as the eruption subsides, the fiery ashes return to their place in the dark caves of the mountain, and there is an eerie quiet that prevails. It is this place of silence that conceals the mask from which the truth can be revealed. The seed of the sorrow was not the anger. It was the hurt—hurt that was lying dormant within the ruins of my mutilated childhood.

I discovered after many volcanic eruptions that I was not angry with my mama. I was agonizingly hurt, wounded to the bone. If she loved me as deeply as she proclaimed, why did she so easily turn me over to the Satan in street clothes? Could that be called love? Was I not precious enough? Was I not worthy enough? Processing the residue of these feelings has been my longest road. It has been filled with the most erratic twists and turns. I often felt as though this solid, cement block of pain had been so deeply hidden and covered with debris that bulldozers would be unable to unearth it and bring it to the light. Still I remained vigilant no matter how painful.

It did not come in an epiphany while walking on a California beach, climbing a Colorado mountain, or sitting in silence under a Bodhi tree. It has taken years, and it has come in stages. With each new revelation, I cried a lifetime of tears for me and another lifetime for her. Slowly with one glimpse and then another, I came to view her through eyes of compassion. I have come to understand that my mama did the best she could with the tools she had, limited though they were. Her strong religious faith, as mighty as it was, still was often impotent to the weight of the sorrow she carried from her own life and from the memories of our shared experiences. I came to selflessly ask how it must have felt for *her* to recall that day she let my hand go leaving me to walk away with Granddaddy. How many times did she lie awake at night recalling that same memory? Did she feel guilt? Shame? Was there just profound regret? I believe it was all of these for both of us. With that knowledge, could I find a space, a tiny slither of a space for forgiveness to enter? I say, yes. The slightest sliver of light did appear. And my journey continued.

More time passed. I moved on in my sobriety carefully carrying these experiences with me. I lived a productive, rich, and full life. And yet, I never lost sight of my need to delve more fully into understanding my own truth and to more fully merge my life with forgiveness and compassion.

With all this, there was still longing in my heart. As I contemplated my future, I came to realize that I had spent my adult life as far away from my roots as I could physically be. I wondered why. The intoxicating, rapid pace of New York City and the alluring lifestyle of Los Angeles had both impacted my life. I had lived them both fully and yet each had taken their toll on me.

During all those years, I had seen my family infrequently during holiday season for short periods of time. What had I missed? Was there now something I needed from them? Did they need something from me? Could my life of longing be fulfilled by the quaint, predictable, charming roots of my childhood? I pondered these queries for some time and soon felt compelled to make a change. I ultimately left my beloved Los Angeles, California, and moved to Nashville, Tennessee. Music City was close enough for me to visit my family often and, yet, far enough away to still maintain my separateness and preserve those barriers I felt I needed to protect myself.

Fourteen

Armageddon Leads to New Beginnings

My long life travels have led me back here to my cozy little cottage in Nashville. It is the third day since my return home. The morning sun peaks through my windows falling softly onto my face. The smell of freshly brewed coffee once again floats up the stairs into my bedroom. Kitty Gracie lies fast asleep nestled sweetly in my down pillow. The conversation Jim and I shared in the small Albany airport is present in my mind. I have worried, I have cried, I have spent hours processing his request. I have diligently explored the recesses of my vast and varied brain searching for my own evidence which I have shared on these pages. It is clear that I have completed all I can complete on my own. I must now look to others to close the circle of this sordid tale.

Long ago someone shared a secret with me that I had kept as promised. My Aunt Dottie's daughter, Diane, had revealed to me many years after we shared our first marijuana joint on the floor of our New

York City apartment that Granddaddy had molested her. I recall being shocked at the time, as I had always thought it was just me. So Diane and I had found a common bond through our well kept secrets. As she shared her story with me that day, I learned that she had reported the Granddaddy molestation to her father and mother. According to her account, her father threatened to get a shotgun and shoot Granddaddy, his own wife's father. I was not privy to any further details. I simply learned that the attempt on Granddaddy's life was aborted and the incident was never mentioned again.

I had always held Diane's secret close to my heart, careful to preserve it. While pondering Jim's question, I recalled the events she had relayed to me. Sadly, Diane had recently passed away from cancer of the spine. I would be unable to gather any further evidence from her. However, if she had indeed told her parents, then her mother, my Aunt Dottie, would remember and could corroborate Diane's story.

I could no longer linger in my sea of fear and suspense. The time was now and the seeker of truth must be me. My tranquil, charming morning would become the starting point of excavation into my painful past. My first call must be to my Aunt Dottie.

My heart raced, my hand shook, and my breath quickened as I dialed her number. Although a part of me hoped she would not answer, the greater part of me was delighted when she did. We chatted of congenial things for some time. Finally, I found the strength to divulge the reason for my call.

"Aunt Dottie, I would like to talk to you about your father," I said as my voice trembled.

I could feel a shift in energy through the phone line. It seemed to me as though she was catching her breath, bracing herself for what was to come. These are my feelings only. She simply said nothing in that short time.

"If you do not want to have this conversation, please let me know. I do not want to cause you any pain," I carefully continued in an effort to relieve her anxiety.

Again, I felt an energy shift, moving this time to a place of openness and compassion.

"No, go ahead. Ask me anything," she said with a gentleness in her voice.

I was now frozen with fear. Speechless. I knew for my own sanity, I must continue the search. I must ask what needed to be asked. As I paced from wall to wall in my bedroom my hands shook. I found it difficult to hold onto the phone. I had to consciously gather my courage. With a deep breath and a shaky voice, I began.

"Aunt Dottie, I was molested by your father from the time I was a very small child, until I went away to college."

I took another deep breath. I had gotten the hard part out, now I could continue.

"I told my brother Jim about it many years ago. He has recently said that he grew up in the same house with me and never saw anything. He feels he would have seen something if it actually had happened. And he did not. "

When Diane told me of her molestation, she was specific with the details of how she told her parents and their reaction to her accusations. With this information in hand, I knew I had to carefully and with grace expose Diane's secret to my Aunt Dottie. It would not be an easy task to discuss the molestation of her first born child, an abuse perpetrated by her own father. I carefully weighed my thoughts before speaking.

"Many years ago, Diane told me that she was also molested by Granddaddy. Jim says he needs some evidence. I am hoping Diane told you and that she is my evidence."

The question had now been asked. Was there evidence, or was it all an illusion? In this shared moment, there was an interminable silence. I could hear Aunt Dottie breathing, choking back her tears.

"You tell your brother, I am the evidence," she said with great poise and at the same time a hint of anger.

I was stunned and completely overcome with emotion. There was nothing, nothing that could have prepared me for her answer. I had to ask myself if I had heard her correctly. As her emotions grew and her heart opened, I knew I had indeed heard her speak her truth. It occurred to me instantly that now there were four: me, Mama, Diane, and Aunt Dottie. This recognition almost took my breath away.

She shared with me that she had never told anyone of the sexual encounters she had endured with her father. She spoke of the ways in which she felt it had inhibited and altered her life. She knew deeply how it had affected her marriage and her ability to give and receive love from her husband and her own children.

The flood gates were now opened, the clear water of revelations and healing flowed freely. We shared our hearts, our tears, and our trust for most of the afternoon. This conversation brought me solace and a deeper understanding of my mother. I could see how these personal damages had played out in our life together. Aunt Dottie then said something I had longed to hear from Mama all my life.

"I am so sorry this happened to you," she simply said as she called my name.

I cried deeply. I cried for her. I cried for me. I cried for Diane and for my dear mama, all victims of one man's dysfunction and disease.

Aunt Dottie and I comforted each other, embraced each other with kind words and shared more deeply our experiences. It was indeed the acceptance I had longed for with Mama that I now was able to receive from her sister. We closed our conversation with love and a deep compassion for each other. I hung up the phone and lay back on my bed, exhausted.

My sweet gray kitty, Gracie, laid her paw on my arm with a yawn and a full body stretch. I gave myself this time, but shortly, the adrenaline in my body prevented me from continuing my moment of repose. I knew I must now call my brother Jim. I dialed his number. He answered quickly.

"I have your evidence," I simply said.

"What is it?" he asked with hesitation in his voice.

"It's Aunt Dottie."

As I revealed the details of my conversation with her, I could tell even my "Doubting Thomas" brother was stunned. His voice softened. He was careful with his responses and his questions. He was a concerned, compassionate listener. I was relieved by his availability and gentleness.

"Me, Mama, Diane, and Aunt Dottie. Now there are four," I counted aloud.

"If there are four, you know there are more." he quietly said.

We reflected upon the possibilities. We named the nine sisters born to our grandparents. Then one by one we counted the daughters birthed by these nine girls. The numbers were staggering. We both realized we had to continue our search for more evidence.

Jim acknowledged that he had a close relationship with one of our other cousins, the daughter of one of Mama's sisters. She was close in age to Jim and had continued a communication with him over the years. He offered to call and broach the subject with her. Still in a state of shock, I gladly handed the task over to him. We terminated our conversation, he in disbelief, and me with a great sense of relief. We had his evidence.

Although Jim never apologized for his disbelief, he fully "joined the team" that day and has been on board ever since.

The following day I went about my duties with a deep feeling of anxiety and fear as I awaited a return call from Jim. Every time my phone rang, my heart sank. Towards the end of the day, while driving home from work, it finally came. I answered with what I can describe only as terror in my voice.

"I have some shocking news," he softly said.

I braced myself for his response.

"She was molested by him, too," he said.

I was so overcome with emotion, my eyes were so filled with tears, I had to pull over on the side of the busy street and park my car. I sat there as all the passersby on their way home from work quickly sped past me. I sat in the dark but for the flashing headlights and wept. Jim did his best to console me. With this new evidence, the magnitude of what was before us began to take hold.

I finally made it home that night exhausted, yet filled with passion. Mama, me, Diane, Aunt Dottie, Aunt D and cousin J. Now there were six confirmed. If there were six, I knew there were many more. I determined that night to find them all.

While still in a state of disbelief the following morning, I received another call from my Aunt Dottie. She had composed a letter to her remaining living sisters. Courage does not adequately describe the sentiments she expressed in those two hand-written pages. Her brave, undaunted and carefully chosen words would be the opening for our family to exhume the darkness that had been lying in the trenches of all our hearts. To me it signaled an opening for our rebirth and the beginning of the light. Here is her letter.

1-13-05
Olympia, Wa.

I am writing this letter to all my sisters – also to (3 of her nieces)
Recently I received a call from Jeanne (Flora's daughter). She finally got the courage to tell someone about her abuse. She first told her brother "Jim", and he, just (at first) would not believe her. She told him her Granddaddy molested her. As soon as she said that she was molested, by her Granddaddy –I blurted out –"Tell him it is the truth – because, I was too." I have been in denial all these years. Jeanne also said her mother, Flora, was molested also. Since the oldest, and the youngest (25 years in-between) were molested, I am wondering, who else out there is in need of help.
I know that my own daughter was a victim, but since I was a victim my self – I could not help her. Even after finally talking to (her other two daughters), I found they knew about Diane, as she had talked to them. After Jeanne told me, it made me able to speak up about it.

I know in my heart that Diane did not blame me, but I wish so much, that I could have had the courage to talk to her.

I think this terrible dark secret in our family, should be let loose and everyone should have release from this denial.

Who else of my sisters, and my nieces are victims?

Maybe you are saying to yourself – "why is she doing this now after so many years. Why did I have to tell this?" – because –we victims need release from this terrible thing that happened to us. I still find it hard to speak of but it helps.

I just hope and pray you are not a victim but if you are – I hope you will not deny it, and you will get help, and talk to me.

I love you all,
Dottie

I was so proud of her. Her willingness to expose the truth even if it meant blowing the family apart was staggering. She hand wrote and mailed each of her sisters the letter. With that Aunt Dottie became my Joan of Arc. Like the beautiful Bastien Lepage painting, she stood alone, against all odds and fought the demons of the deeds of her father.

Her courage deeply inspired me. I knew exactly what I must now do. I had to dig into the next level of females in our family and look for more victims. I made a plan to call all the female children of my mama's sisters. There were many. These were my cousins who had played together 'round that sprawling oak tree. We had picked the blackberries for Grandma to make into cobbler. We had gathered in the living room for the singing of church hymns, run along the railroad tracks, pulled figs out of the water trough in the backyard of the old farm and held hands in prayer before all those Thanksgiving dinners.

I told Jim of my plan. He generously offered to gather all the telephone numbers so that I could continue my search. Within an hour I had them all. Since my work schedule had prevented me from attending family reunions, I had not spoken to most of them for years. I was nervous

Armageddon Leads to New Beginnings

about making cold calls to these virtual strangers especially since the topic of conversation was so unpleasant and potentially revealing. I reflected on Aunt Dottie's letter and the courage she exhibited even though she was sure to face enormous criticism from her sisters. I would not allow my own fear to cripple me in the presence of her undaunted heroism. In no particular order I chose my first name and picked up the phone.

With each ring, my heart beat a little faster, until finally she answered. I began the conversation by identifying myself. We then shared a casual "long-time-no-hear" greeting. When the small talk was completed, I announced the purpose for my call. I was careful to consider her feelings.

"I am sorry if this is painful for you but I have some questions about Granddaddy."

"Go ahead," she said with some hesitancy.

"I was molested by him for years. I now know that my mother, Diane, and Aunt Dottie were also molested by him. I believe there are others amongst us. Do you know anything?"

"He raped me under the railroad pass," my first caller responded with anger in her voice.

I recall feeling faint. The use of such a violent word to describe her experience brought a more profound reality to our darkness. I was once again stunned to learn that now there were seven.

"It was a long time ago and I have tried to put it all behind me," she later remarked.

"Did your mother know about your rape?" I asked.

"No. I have never told her." I remember thinking that our wall of silence continued.

We closed our conversation with warmth and great compassion for each others experiences. Then there were seven. I was not alone. She was not alone. We were not alone.

At this point, I felt much like a caged tiger, panting and pacing back and forth. I wanted to scream, "What the hell is happening here? Is this possible?" In my frenzy of excitement I searched for the next number on my list. Then I realized I had best calm down before making another call. I sat on the side of my bed and took a deep breath. Within minutes I was more centered. I picked up the phone and dialed her number. I began the conversation in much the same way as the first, casual greeting, small talk, and heartfelt concern for the question I was about to ask.

"Do you have any experience with Granddaddy?"

This younger cousin was slower to answer. I sensed she was in great conflict and was agonizing over her response.

Finally she said in a whisper, "I have never told anyone. Yes, he did it to me, too."

Her sadness ran deep, and yet I sensed an exhilarating feeling of relief. Her secret had now been exposed. Astonishingly enough, now there were eight. I was not alone. She was not alone. We were not alone.

It was almost impossible to contain all the sorrow, shock, and shame that ran through my mind and body. It became clear to me now that, yes, "This was possible." It was possible that one man alone had created this devastation quietly and unnoticed for two generations. I was emboldened. Now the pacing, panting tiger turned into one that gnashed its teeth with determination and passion to capture every ounce of evidence. I picked up the phone and dialed another number.

My next dear cousin responded to my same query with a profound sense of loss.

"I thought all my life I was the only one. I have suffered all by myself."

Then in a burst of anger she shouted, "I hate the bastard."

I was relieved to hear some genuine acrimony expressed. I shouted it right back at her. "I hate that bastard too." I suspect we were not alone in that sentiment. Now there were nine.

Again, I was almost overcome with the magnitude of the responses from my heart-broken cousins. I reflected on our innocence when last we really knew each other. Unbeknown to us at the time, we each carried the bond of silence. An agreement we either made with him or one that we determined to keep within our own hearts. Either way, we had all suffered. But no more. I continued with the calls.

My next sweet cousin replied in desperation after I asked the question.

"Yes, he molested me too. Please don't tell my husband and children. They do not know. I have never told anyone."

I knew enough to realize that even though she had never told her husband, the scars of her abuse were certainly felt by him. I imagine them to be experienced in much the same way as described by Aunt Dottie. I knew in my heart that I had missed out on so much with my own husband. There was a richness, a fullness that the scars of my abuse had prevented me from achieving. So in the end, husbands and wives had all missed out on intimacy and a closeness that only fear prevents. I was filled with compassion.

Now there were ten. I was not alone. She was not alone. We were not alone.

The day was growing long and I was weary. Yet there were others to call before I rested. I continued with tenacious fervor. My next caller was angrier than the last. She provided more details of Granddaddy's boldness and overt perverse behavior. She described several encounters with him one summer.

"He used to lie down in the bushes in the backyard where we played. He would unzip his pants and pull out his penis. He'd wave it at me and say, 'Look at the worm, look at the worm'."

Granddaddy's level of indignity was stunning. I reflected back to those summer days when the boys and girls played together among the blackberry bushes. I wondered how it was that only the girls were witness to this behavior. It was beyond unbelievable. And yet, I had to acknowledge that now there were eleven. I was not alone. She was not alone. We were not alone.

As I continued my quest, I was met with my first opposition. I began with the usual casual conversation then moved easily and quickly into the purpose of my call. I shared with my cousin the evidence I had discovered. She gasped for air and with the roar of an angry lion she screamed,

"Are you telling me that our granddaddy molested you and his own grandchildren? I will not believe it. I will not believe it."

I was shocked by her reaction. I naively expected everyone to respond with openness and availability. Her reaction awakened my compassion. I realized the power of what I was telling her. She was hearing the "evidence" for the first time. I thought it best to terminate the conversation.

"I apologize for this call. I am so sorry. I did not mean to hurt you."

As my search continued, there were others who simply slammed the phone down, refusing to engage in any conversation with me regarding our granddaddy. I have come to understand their inability to take in the magnitude of what was being revealed in our family. I also understood that my desire for the truth would not always be welcomed. I learned to accept that.

I also learned that one person's fear must not be a deterrent to my quest for authenticity. I continued, careful not to hurt those who were too deeply wounded to even know they were scarred.

"I was raped by him … many times," my next responder said through her tears.

Then there were twelve.

The day finally ended. The calls were now complete. I lay back on my bed, closed my tired eyes, and lifted up a prayer of thanksgiving and gratitude. Thanks for giving me the courage to ask the questions. Thanks for the honesty and valor of those who had this day shared their sorrow for the first time. Thanks for the opportunity to reveal the truth. Thanks for the challenge of the experience—one that I now see has stroked my life with beautiful hues and influenced my relationships with unique and varied shapes. It was one of the most profound, invigorating, exhausting, enlightening, and uplifting days of my life. I was not alone. She was not alone. We were not alone.

The following day, I shared with my Aunt Dottie all that I had learned from my fellow survivors. She too had uncovered more from her sisters. Only one was willing to discuss with her what had happened. The general response was "it was a long time ago. We have to move on." Others responded with enormous anger. She maintained her reserve and still managed to get the answers she wanted.

With her help, our numbers now jumped to a staggering thirteen, then fourteen, and fifteen. As we continued our search for evidence, we finally came to a total of seventeen known members of our family who had been violated by this one man. *Seventeen.* I was not alone. They were not alone. We were not alone. None of us were left in the silence of our dark and burdensome secrets. The warm, soothing light of disclosure had been shed on each of our stories.

These recent revelations opened another door to understanding and finding more peace in my relationship with Mama. I more deeply grasped the pain she carried. How is one capable of protecting others when they too are vulnerable, exposed, and unprotected? In the lineage of our family, being the first born to Grandma and Granddaddy, Mama may have been his first victim. In that sense, she carried the weight of all those who followed her, a burden far too great for any child to sustain.

I came to love her more deeply than I ever knew was possible. All those barriers that prevented me from fully embracing her or allowing her to fully embrace me were removed. It was as though I had been chipping away at those grand impediments with a tiny spoon since first we met on her 42nd birthday. We had climbed Mount Everest together. We swam the mighty seas. Now here we stood on the other side of it all, looking out from our highest peak.

As I continued gathering information, I quickly came to see that the forgiveness I had once felt for Granddaddy's demons became a fleeting memory. Armed now with scores of victims, my rage reemerged with a vengeance. It was somehow simpler when it was just me. With my entire family now involved, it became a momentous task. His demons were now darker, deeper, more daunting and profoundly more dangerous.

All those times I was returned to the living room after he had his way with me, unbeknown to me, he was picking up another young child to take to the woods. He was a man so consumed by his addiction that it permitted him to sexually abuse seventeen of his own children and grandchildren. (Seventeen is the confirmed number. I believe there are more among those who refused my calls.) What kind of demonic villain lived inside that mind and body? Having myself lived inside an addiction, I had an understanding of the hold it can have on one's soul. And yet, I did not want to let him go. My demon within surmised that by holding onto my rage, he would suffer and pay for his deeds.

Many nights I was awake until dawn, unable to let the stories go. There was no space in my rational mind for understanding of how this kind of abuse could have gone unabated for so many years—two generations. In all that time, no one said one word until I made that call to Aunt Dottie. Now the flood gates opened and we were drowning in the stench of one man's misdeeds. I was choking myself to death while still alive, nauseated daily and losing weight. I was consumed with rage and could feel it pulsing through my blood. The only place of solace was walking among the beautiful, green hills of Tennessee. I spent as much time outside as I could in the freedom and beauty of nature. In God's Space.

Then one day it occurred to me that Granddaddy was gone. He would not be making another appearance in any of our lives. From an early age, I had been taught in Sunday School that "sinners" would find their "just punishment in purgatory." As far as I know, no one has ever returned from the fires of hell to report on the conditions there, so I could not be certain that there was actually such a place for folks like my granddaddy. It was certainly a matter of faith, and at this point mine was shaky at best. In the end, it mattered little whether he was suffering or not. I knew that I was and that was no longer acceptable. I realized the futility of needing to know that he was paying for his sins. I came to recognize that the only one suffering from that decision would be me. I would not give him that. I would instead give myself freedom.

After I freed myself, I once again unlocked my compassion and let him go. I forgave his demons, more desperate and malicious than first I knew. There are those in my family who will not forgive him. I understand. I did find, however, that once I freed him, I further freed myself. I win.

Several days after these events, breathing fresh air and feeling great joy in my heart, I took a walk in the familiar woods near my Tennessee home. The tall, majestic trees were just beginning to shed their autumn leaves of gold and red. Multi-colored butterflies flitted by resting for brief reposes on delicate wild flowers. Many and varied birds blended their songs and lifted them into the cool fall air. Suddenly the magnificence of the universe rushed over me, engulfing me with a knowing, a peace, a profound recognition of the Divine Order that is our lives. I knew none of this had been an accident. As my heart soared, I felt Mama's presence in that gentle breeze, in those flitting butterflies. I heard her rich, soprano voice in the lyrical serenade of the songbirds. It was as if she had been waiting for me to discover and unveil all the fullness of our family disease. She was the first to experience it. It was my duty, responsibility and great honor to end it by shedding the light on our total eclipse of the sun. Symbolically, I felt the warmth of her loving most gentle hand reach out to embrace my long awaited, open arms. Even in her death with me all alone in the woods, at long last my mama became my advocate.

I have asked myself if this is what forgiveness looks like. My answer is that forgiveness is whatever brings solace, takes away the pain, eases the pressure, lifts the fog from one's eyes, brings peace when you recall a person's face, and allows one to move forward with confidence and grace. Forgiveness is freedom for the offended. In turn, forgiveness also leaves the offender on their own so that fate can take hold.

It has astounded me, though, that this light of forgiveness would so thoroughly flow only after the excavation of the poison that had permeated the hearts and souls of the women in my family, a poison that had altered all of our lives and profoundly shaped our destiny for generations. From this I have learned that in order to intimately heal, one must go to the depths of the root, the source of the evil and without equivocation, yank it out like a bind weed. Some of us have done just that.

All of my incest-surviving cousins have traversed their own paths since the revelations of the pervasiveness of our grandfather's exploits. Some have chosen to replant the weed and simply continue with their lives. Several daughters in the same family attempted to speak with their mother regarding the abuse. She acknowledged her own molestation as a child, remarked that it was a long time ago, and refused further conversation with her daughters and any attempt to assuage their pain. She subsequently passed away taking to her grave any meaningful dialogue or hope for one-on-one forgiveness with her own children.

As I watched my cousins struggle with this lost opportunity, I was once again confronted with the multiple and diverse layers that are required for true forgiveness. I was enraged that all of our mothers, themselves victims of the abuse, had not been more vigilant in protecting their own daughters. I was being asked to dig deeper, understand more, and hold compassion from a grander elevation that in the moment appeared beyond my reach. It has taken time. It has taken patience and it has taken compassion for my own process. And yet with more quiet thought, careful reflection, and awakened empathy, in my own way, I have come to forgive them all. I came to see that our soul-scars matched. This is what opened my heart.

I find still that I am not done. What about the men? Where were they? What did they see? What did they know? Did they walk away too? Where are they now? I still do not know. I fear the secret remains locked in shame from them. Perhaps I will find the courage one day to take up the cause and shed the light of healing on them all. Until then, I commend my brother Jim. He recognizes that he was blind to all that occurred "right in the same house." Now he stands tall as our champion. In reality, without his doubt, none of us would have been able to shed the light on our darkness. As a family we found goodness in his questioning. I am eternally grateful.

With all the focus on forgiving others, I found in the end the most difficult to forgive was me, my mind, my heart, my soul. I had failed to recognize the depth of Mama's love for me. With that oversight, I am certain I missed many of her gifts. I had to dig deep and search with a careful eye to find my peace with this. On those days now when I long to hear her voice, even after all these years, I must acknowledge a sadness that lingers on and lurks in the darkness. My work continues.

Let it not be thought that once I came to these understandings that all was good and right in my world. It is on some days and not so on others. Healing is a journey. A long, winding, bumpy journey to grace. Although I do not consciously recall the events of my childhood often, I can see the effects in my daily life. I am more guarded than most, vigilant in protecting my feelings from others. I am terrified to give love fully, although, I work at it in all my relationships. Through the action of doing, my fear has lessened. I am making great strides. Finding myself alone with an unknown male remains a source of great discomfort. I have often panicked when I have to schedule a workman for a routine maintenance on a household appliance. Often when I see a small child with her grandfather in a department store, I will follow them through the aisles making sure she is safe with him. Overcoming my "victim nature" has been a conscious effort. I have learned that I must choose to see myself as the victor rather than being at the mercy of another. I do have that choice and I exercise it daily.

I have found peace in releasing my judgment of those I feel betrayed me. Yes, my granddaddy's actions were unconscionable. The silence of our mothers was inexcusable. However, what I do with their behaviors determines my success or failure in life. Horrific as it was, none of them is responsible for my feelings. Only I have that authority. Thus it becomes my journey. Only I can pave the way before me. The scars remain for sure. I now choose to wear them as symbols of my triumph over darkness. I am victorious because I continue on, carrying my own baggage, not holding anyone else responsible for it, and enjoying the ride. It is a beautiful experience without which my life would be less remarkable.

No one knows what my sweet, toothless grandma knew as she birthed eleven children and maneuvered about that sprawling old farm house. As a child, late at night, Aunt Dottie recalls on numerous occasions hearing her mother cry out, "No, No." I will not allow myself to imagine what she endured in the dark of night for all those years.

For the others who remain silent, I say shame is nefarious by its sheer nature. It destroys its prey from within. I believe it still has some of our family by a choke hold. May your silence soothe and comfort you. I choose to release this noose. I walk along side my Aunt Dottie and those heroic cousins who had the courage to expose their truth.

There are those who deny and refuse to acknowledge the existence of any improprieties perpetrated upon the children by our father/grandfather. It is not easy to be made whole again when so many pieces lay shattered and strewn about. I must now leave them to swim alone in their sea of denial.

There are many who are in the Spirit world, those who took their secret to their graves, those who seemingly have no voice. I will speak here for them.

There are those who have cursed me for shedding light on this darkness. And, yet, I must speak here for them.

Then there are those who now read the words on these pages, those who silently and with deep shame endure the abuse and betrayal of their own incest. Until they find their voice, may I speak here for them.

And for my *Sistahs*. you have walked through it all with me and still stand by my side. When I was crazy you remained compassionate.

When I was sad, you understood and yet made me laugh. When I lost ground, you gathered 'round me and helped me up the mountain. You are my "soul mates." I am beyond grateful and profoundly blessed by your presence in my life.

And for my betrayer, my granddaddy, smoker of cigarettes and slayer of innocence, may you be released from your chain of addiction, and may God have mercy on your soul.

For my dear, beloved Mama, there are no relationships as deep, as complicated, nor as eternal. I love you with all my heart. Our story has now been told. In its telling, may you find peace as I have.

THE END

Made in the USA
Charleston, SC
11 June 2015